HIGH
TECHNOLOGY

HIGH TECHNOLOGY

STEVEN SCHNEIDER

Contemporary Books, Inc.
Chicago

Library of Congress Cataloging in Publication Data

Schneider, Steven, 1951-
  High technology.

  Bibliography: p.
  Includes index.
  1. Mountaineering—Equipment and supplies.
I. Title.
GV200.15.S36   1980   688.7'6'522   79-8744
ISBN 0-8092-7315-2
ISBN 0-8092-7314-4 pbk.

Published by Contemporary Books, Inc.
180 North Michigan Avenue, Chicago, Illinois 60601
Manufactured in the United States of America
Library of Congress Catalog Card Number: 79-8744
International Standard Book Number: 0-8092-7315-2 (cloth)
                                   0-8092-7314-4 (paper)

Published simultaneously in Canada by
Beaverbooks
953 Dillingham Road
Pickering, Ontario L1W 1Z7
Canada

To Rosalie

Contents

Acknowledgments

I would like to express my appreciation to all those who contributed to this book in one way or another, including Lisa Airhart of P.G.B. International Trading Company, Ltd.; Bill Ashley of Synergy Works; Giuseppe Cereghini of Euro-Linea; Ron Etherington of Vista Thermal Products, Ltd.; Bill Forrest of Forrest Mountaineering; John Hiffman of Cedar River Mountaineering; Ed Leeper of Leeper Mountaineering Equipment; Nancy Listor of Rivendell Mountain Works; Mike Lowe of Lowe Alpine Systems; Ernst Meinhart of Anderson and Thompson Ski Company; Denny Moorhouse of Clogwyn Climbing Gear, Ltd.; Pierre Muffat of Sacs Millet; Lillian Simond of Simond Mountaineering Equipment; Alvin Stallman of Pak Foam Products; A. B. Walker of Tog 24 Textral Manufacturing; and Alan Waterhouse of Troll Products. I would also like to especially thank my friend and fellow climbing guide, Chris Rowins, for his expert judgment and assistance.

Introduction

The age of mountaineering has arrived in America. American climbers are now setting standards for the world to watch and follow and American climbs now have a worldwide reputation for quality.

A typical spring afternoon in Yosemite sees climbers from Europe, England, and elsewhere on the globe preparing their ropes for El Cap, The Sentinel, Half-Dome, and other Yosemite walls. A team of crack Soviet mountaineers has visited the Shawangunks, the Tetons, the Valley, and the Cascades as part of an international exchange program sponsored by the American Alpine Club. French climbers, who normally would winter in Chamonix, are drawn by the reputation of New England's Cannon Cliff and have climbed the VMC Direct in winter. The prestigious British magazine, *Mountain,* has been publishing more and more articles on major American climbs. These are but a few indications that the peaks of America are receiving proper attention.

In days past, climbing, like tennis, was reserved for the upper class. But the children of America's melting pot have now joined the ranks of early European aristocrats by venturing forth into the world's vertical wildernesses. The increasing affluence of the American middle class and an abundance of leisure time have made climbing possible for plain folks. They are able to take advantage of the continual progress in high technology by attempting climbs and routes that were previously unclimbable.

The mountains were once the domain of a few intrepid adventurers—fearless men. Today, climbing seems to be becoming as popular as sandlot baseball was in the thirties and forties. And the increasing interest in mountaineering has created a demand for equipment, both American-made and imported. Scores of shops have sprouted up in cities and small towns to supply and service this equipment. In fact, today, the most significant mountaineering advances seem to be in the equipment used, rather than in the climbs themselves. In mountaineering, as in so many aspects of our space-age society, technology is leading the way. New items, with amazingly innovative qualities, are being introduced into the market every year, always improving the ability of climbers to seek new challenges. From the walls of Yosemite to the crystal cascades of Colorado and New England ice, the American mountaineer has benefited from rethought, redesigned, improved, or re-created tools, clothing, and equipment. Clothing and accessories are warmer, and tools are more intricate and useful; yet clothing, accessories, and tools are all lighter in weight. Climbers are able to move more quickly and freely over difficult terrain.

This book offers a discussion of the latest and best items available on today's market, in the author's opinion. It is not meant to be a comprehensive discussion of *all* available equipment, or of *all* types of mountaineering gear. Rather, its aim is to present information on the best of the tried-and-true equipment and on some exciting new products that point the way to mountaineering in the 1980s and beyond.

Protection Systems: Pitons

A Little Background History

Pitons were relatively unheard of before 1925. Primitive protection devices devised by climbers were large steel nails banged into the rock wall with the protruding end bent under to form a hook to which the climbing rope could be attached. The earliest known use of these devices in the United States was in the late 1800s on a first ascent of the Grand Teton by the Owen Spalding route. Much later, the bent nails that Spalding used were discovered at the base of the route and are now on display at Teton National Park.

Bent nails came into common use during the 1920s in Europe. Nonetheless, because nails were still suspect, one of the early users, climbing guide Alfred Couttet, made his clients promise they would not tell anyone they were using them.

Soon, climbers began to hand forge their own pitons,

with a closed eye at one end. These "rock nails," though still primitive, were a little more advanced than the earlier bent hooks. The eye provided much better protection than a bent hook because the rope could not slip out. The "rock nails" were made from soft iron, which could be molded to the shape of the cracks in the walls.

Pitons were at first viewed as unnecessary, unwarranted, and undesirable. Climbers resisted using them. However, as younger climbers came along, pitons gained popularity and were eventually accepted as a valid and valuable protection device.

It was not until the late 1950s that hard metal was used in forging pitons. John Salathé designed the hard-metal piton, named it the Lost Arrow, and introduced it to the American climbing market. This was the first commercially produced piton in America and was a major step in the advancement of both piton-craft and climbing in general. In 1959, Yvon Chouinard introduced his Horizontal Knifeblade and Bugaboo pitons, also made of hard metal, which resisted the deformation caused by repeated use common to the soft-metal European pitons.

Chouinard and Tom Frost formed the Great Pacific Iron Works Company in Ventura, California. Their new, hard-metal pins (pitons) made possible most of the major climbs in Yosemite Valley and pushed the standard of American climbing into the world arena. (Their Great Pacific Iron Works catalog, by the way, is a work of art, and essential reading for anyone serious about technical mountaineering. It contains a wealth of information about the proper use of equipment, techniques and tricks for climbing, and good discussions of mountaineering gear. The catalog is available for one dollar.)

Choosing and Using Pitons

Before one selects any protection device, he should

know that alternative devices are available. As Bill Forrest says, "When the experienced climber needs protection beyond his physical and mental resources, he attempts to fashion it from natural features. When they are absent, he places chocks; if these are inadequate, he drives pitons."

Until 1965, the only protection devices available were pitons. All of the large major ascents in Yosemite, the climbs in New Hampshire, in Colorado, and in the Olympics, required the use of pitons to anchor climbers to the wall safely.

Whichever protection system a climber uses, he should know its potential weaknesses and strengths. Piton craft cannot be learned in a day or two. It takes many, many climbs before all of the options in using pitons are understood. We recommend that climbers practice with their pitons on small climbs before using them on higher mountains. The best instructions for use of pitons are contained in Yvon Chouinard's catalog. Since I can't improve on them, I'll include them here:

METHOD OF DRIVING

The most common error made in the use of alloy steel pitons is over-driving them. This destroys the piton as well as the rock. Optimum holding power comes not from beating the piton to death, but from sophisticated placing so that under a load it will wedge itself and resist shifting. The section of crack that best provides this natural resistance to rotation may be a locally wider spot that constricts above or below or it may be a straighter section that grips the piton securely near each end of the blade. In a perfect placement the rugosities of the crack will provide a resistance to downward rotation approaching that which is enjoyed in horizontal cracks. By way of contrast, a poor placement exists where only a single high spot contacts the blade and provides an unwanted pivot point. If the available piton will not go in all the way to the eye, leverage on it can be reduced by tying off with a Hero Loop. Testing with the hammer is an important part of correct driving. In a much less violent way, testing is identical with the first steps of the removal procedure, and as such gives an indication of the holding power of the piton. All pitons found in place should be tested in this manner before use.

The complete method of placement is summarized as follows: First, select the piton size for the crack and then locate the section of the crack that best fits the piton. (Depending upon its length and taper, the piton should normally allow one-half to three-quarters of the blade to be inserted into the crack before driving.) Pound the piton in only part way, then with one or two light downward blows on the head to see how well it is in, and how well it resists shifting. Then drive more according to the results of the test, and retest with another downward blow (vertical crack assumed) until the piton appears adequately solid in its resistance to shifting. Restrain the urge to give it that one extra blow—this is the one that will make the piton difficult to remove and cause it and the rock to become unnecessarily damaged in the process. If, however, a perfect placement is not possible, then the best security can of course be obtained from a really hard-driven piton, particularly in vertical cracks.

The overall speed of the party is enhanced considerably if pitons are placed no firmer than required to do the job, and with an eye toward removal as well as holding power, because the total time spent on any piton is the sum of placement time and removal time. Theoretically, pitons used only for artificial aid need hold little more than body weight. Anchors and protection pitons may be required to hold as much as 3,000 pounds. Much less driving is required when the crack fits the piton—and therefore, removal is easier and piton and crack life is prolonged.

NAILING FLEXIBLE FLAKES

When driving more than one piton behind the same flexible flake or slab, caution must be exercised so that each succeeding piton does not expand the crack and loosen the preceding ones. To minimize expansion, the use of chocks is particularly recommended. They are inherently more stable than pitons, and therefore can provide more holding power with less expansion of the crack. Chocks can enhance both climber safety and preservation of flakes and slabs.

Alternatively, use long bladed pitons with little taper and place them in locally wider sections of the crack that provide natural resistance to rotation. Insert the piton with the fingers about three-fourths of its length then pound just enough to hold without overly expanding the crack. Begin driving the next piton then clip the climbing rope into it before driving it home; or clip into the new piton via an étrier or runner in case the one you are standing in comes out. With a bit of luck the piton you are driving will hold your fall.

When nailing underneath the lower edge of a flake, try to place the piton at an angle to the direction of pull rather than straight up. This way, if the crack should expand, hopefully the piton will shift a bit and cunningly jam itself rather than pulling straight out.

METHOD OF REMOVING

The usual mistake in removing is not hitting the piton far enough to the side in each direction, but just tapping it back and forth near the center of its range of travel. The proper method is to hit the piton in one direction until it will absolutely go no further—then hit it some more before driving it back in the opposite direction. Use plenty of force but remember that most of the damage to the crack happens during the removal stage. Keep aware and avoid the breaking off of flexible flakes and rugosities along the edges of the crack. Avoid damage to the piton by directing the removal blows to the neck area rather than the anvil of the piton. In flared cracks and when the étrier is left clipped in to prevent dropping the piton, the blows are applied to the neck with the blunt pick end of the Yosemite Hammer.

Because pitons are tapered they will work themselves out. But if a piton is tenaciously gripped by an expanding flake it can usually be removed by applying the flexible flake technique in reverse: drive a thicker piton nearby and purposely expand the crack. Also, the étrier can be attached and pulled steadily out while the piton is pounded from side to side. By applying this method the piton will often fly out giving you a good smack in the face.

Rather than damaging a piton or destroying a crucial flake or crack while trying to remove it, the piton should be left in place for others to use. Succeeding parties must become aware of the problem too, and employ wisdom and restraint in the removal of necessary fixed pitons that will precipitate further damage to the route.

I would like to echo Chouinard's words and urge that, whenever possible, pitons should be left in place once inserted into a crack. Repeated pounding in and removal of pins scars and defaces rocks badly. In some cases, cracks that used to be ¼-inch wide have grown as wide as 1 inch. If a pin is necessary, make sure it is well placed, and then leave it in place. Climbers should also leave in place those pitons they find already on the wall. If a pin is found to be loose, a thoughtful climber will re-drive it in securely.

I have recently experienced a situation where, after establishing a first ascent on Cannon Cliff, we returned to reclimb it and found that the route had been completely cleaned of all pitons. We later learned that the pins had been removed out of pure maliciousness. To say the least, this is poor sportsmanship; but, fortunately, such actions on the part of climbers are rare.

Care and Maintenance

A piton is a strong and durable implement. Once pounded into a crack, it can be left for years without concern that the metal will give way. If, however, a piton is exposed to a great deal of water over a period of time, it will eventually rust to the point where it is no longer usable. Do not worry about surface rust; this will not reduce the effectiveness of your pins. If you are going to store your pitons for a long period of time, spray them with a coating of oil or WD-40 to protect the metal.

A piton blade will sometimes bend after numerous uses. We've found that by placing the blade in a vise and tightening the vise a blade can be straightened without noticeable loss of strength. Any burrs or nicks on the blade may be removed with a metal file.

If you should notice small fatigue cracks appearing in your pitons, they should be retired and replaced with new ones.

Market Update

Pitons are manufactured and distributed by several equipment companies in the United States. We'll discuss a few of the best available.

Chouinard originally handcrafted his pitons in California. Now his Lost Arrow pitons are being manufactured to his specifications by the Interalp Company in Italy. No major design changes have been made, and Chouinard pins are the standard in American climbing.

Clog pitons are made from nickel-chrome-molybdenum steel and will last through many years of constant pounding. Pins by Clog include the Angle and the King Pin. The King Pin is basically the same design as the traditional Lost Arrow, and is available in a variety of sizes: short thin, long thin, short medium, long medium, long thick, and extra-long. I've used Clogs for the past five years and am extremely happy with their performance. They hold up remarkably well and are an excellent choice.

Probably the most interesting and original design for a piton was developed and manufactured by Ed Leeper of Boulder, Colorado. Using chromium-molybdenum alloy, he created a piton in a Z shape. These are referred to as

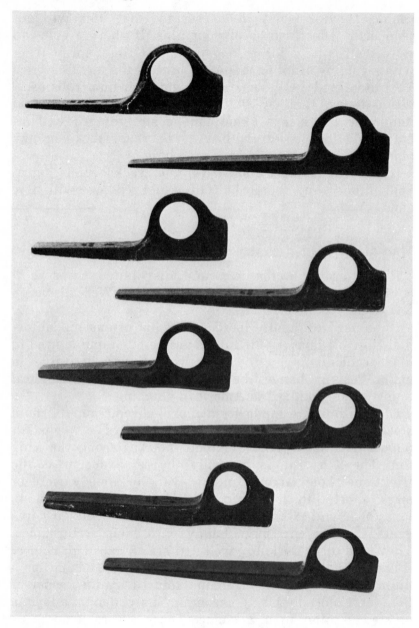

Above and opposite, *Chouinard pitons.*
(Courtesy of Great Pacific Iron Works.)

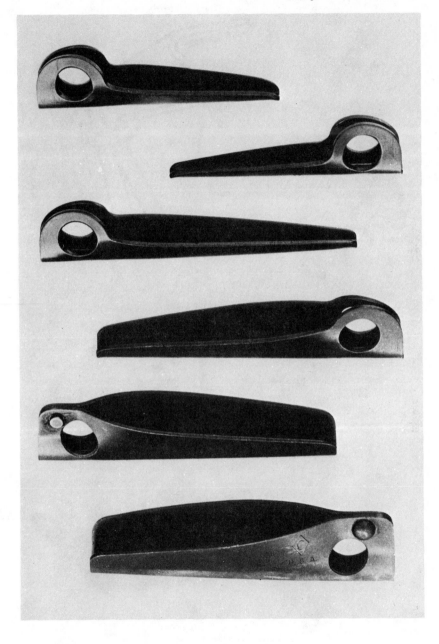

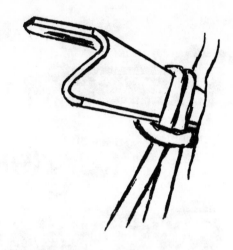

Leeper Z pitons.
(Courtesy of Ed Leeper.)

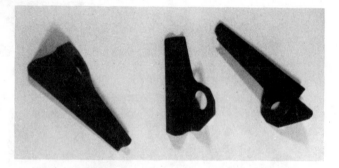

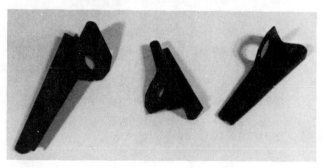

"Leeper's Z" pitons. When properly placed, the Z pin is probably the strongest pin for any given position. They are particularly strong for aid climbing and for tying off the pin. No matter how far into the crack the Z pin is placed, by tying off close to the rock, you have a remarkably strong anchor. I have taken falls from poor placements of Chouinard and Clog pins. Maybe because I place the Z pins better, I have never yet popped one out of the wall during a fall. I almost always carry a few Leeper Zs on my rack, and recommend them highly.

Ed Leeper also created what he calls an Antipiton by reversing the taper of his Z pin. The Antipiton was designed to be stacked with a regular piton at right angles to it, and does not require a hammer for placement. Downward force on the eye (to which the rope is clipped) causes the pair to tighten in the crack as the Antipiton moves. The action is like that of a well-placed nut, except that the Antipiton works best in smooth, straight cracks.

Antipiton placement requires skill and care, just as does any clean climbing placement. Anchors should be doubled and tripled for safety. The main point of technique is that the intersection of the piton and Antipiton should not be too close to the tip of the Antipiton because the Antipiton may move as much as two inches or more when a fall is caught. With a large force, it will move more than you expect. That movement can be reduced, however, if the piton is hammered into place.

A long hero loop of ½-inch webbing should join the eye of the stacked piton to the carabiner clipped into the Antipiton (to avoid losing it). It should be long enough not to pull the piton out of position when the Antipiton moves in a fall.

When stacking an Angle piton with the Antipiton, the Angle piton should be placed with the edges against the rock and the rounded side against the Antipiton. Otherwise the anchor can be dragged out of place in a fall. With

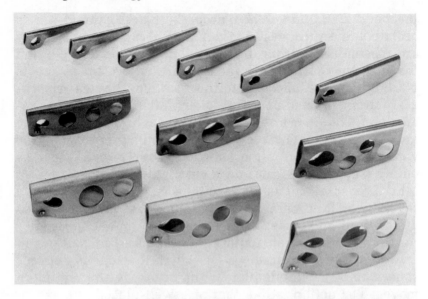

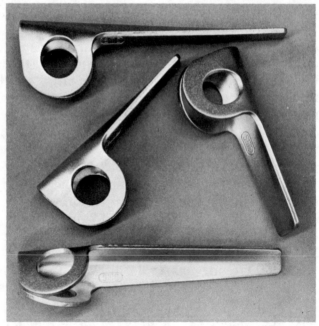

SMC pitons.
(Courtesy of Seattle Manufacturing Corporation.)

luck and skill, Antipiton placements will sometimes hold several thousand pounds. The Antipiton is no longer being manufactured, but many stores in the United States still carry them. If aid climbing is your thing, a set of Antipitons could give you protection that conventional nut or pin placement does not offer.

SMC (Seattle Manufacturing Corporation) offers short and long pitons with a unique channel design; they are particularly good for permanent placement. The shorter one is almost impossible to remove once inserted into a crack. The SMC pins will fit cracks up to 3 inches wide.

The Simond Company in France offers pitons in four models. The *Piton de Rocher* is an offset design and offers very good protection in especially thin cracks. The Simond U pin is designed to fill the gap between a conventional blade pin and an Angle pin. Both the *Piton de Rocher* and the U pin are made from soft, malleable steel.

Two hard steel pins are available from Simond. One is in the conventional Angle design, available in four sizes. The most useful Simond piton for American climbing, however, is the Multiroc, which is made in the Universal shape. It allows a carabiner to be easily clipped into its

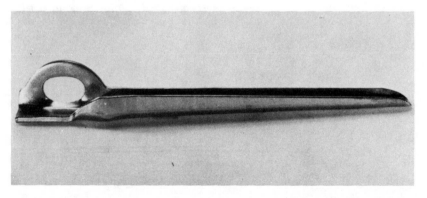

Simond Piton de Rocher.
(Courtesy of ETS Claudius Simond et fils.)

eye, regardless of the configuration in which the pin is placed. All Simond pins are available in the United States, but in limited quantities.

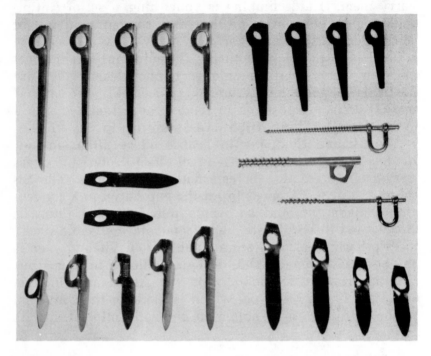

Simond pins.
(Courtesy of ETS Claudius Simond et fils.)

2

Protection Systems: Nuts

A Little Background History

The first climbing nuts, also called chockstones or chocks, came not from the machines of man but from the environment. In the 1940s and 1950s, as climbers in England walked to the base of their climbs they made it a practice to gather stones of various sizes. These stones could be wedged into a crack and a rope passed around them. Thus, a perfectly natural protection system was devised.

Climbers soon realized that a common hexagonal nut, found in a machine shop, would be an ideal replacement for a stone. It even had an advantage; the climbing rope could be passed through the center hole of the nut after the internal threads were filed away with a rat-tail file.

In the early 1960s two British climbers, Alan Waterhouse and Paul Seddon began experimenting with nuts manufactured specifically for climbing. They produced the first commercially made climbing hex-nut. Experiments with different shapes were conducted. Circular nuts, wedge-shaped nuts, and hexagonals were tested to fit into cracks of varying shapes. The MOAC Company in Great Britain devised a wedge-shaped nut, later referred to simply as the MOAC, which became widely used. The Peck Company produced a rounded nut that varied in length from 1 to 2 inches and had two curved surfaces. These were made with drilled holes for slinging the rope through.

The Peck Company also devised the first cable nuts, ingenious little devices that solved a number of problems. Cable nuts are small, to fit into tiny cracks. Of course, when nuts are made smaller their holes must also be smaller, which prevents a sturdy climbing rope from being passed through. Nuts attached to strong, yet narrow, cables solved this problem, and gave the climber a longer reach for inserting the nuts into cracks. When reaching to insert a nut that is slung on a supple rope, the rope will flop over; whereas a wire cable will remain straight. This, in effect, gives the climber's arm a few more inches.

In 1965 Royal Robbins was climbing the Bastille Crack in El Dorado Canyon with British climber, Anthony (Tony) Greenbank. Tony was using the Peck "Crackers," and several kinds of wedge nuts designed by Brian Henderson, a leading British crag specialist. Robbins watched with amazement as Tony easily dropped the nuts into place and continued his climb. Robbins tried them himself and was so pleased with them that he immediately began to import them into the United States. He became the first American advocate of the use of climbing nuts in place of pitons.

Yvon Chouinard also discovered that nuts made an ascent quicker and easier. Using the design of the original MOAC and Brian Henderson's wedge nuts, he produced the first American wedge nut and called it the Stopper. (All wedge nuts are now referred to as stoppers.) These two men, Robbins and Chouinard, are essentially respon-

Chouinard Stoppers.
(Courtesy of Great Pacific Iron Works.)

sible for introducing clean climbing to the walls of the United States.

In Yosemite Valley, during the late 1960s, many of the rock faces were climbed with nuts used in conjunction with pitons. Then bolder climbers started to use a rack of all nuts. Further design changes in British nuts and the availability of various nuts from Chouinard and Robbins made it possible for most existing technical climbs in the United States to be done with nuts rather than pitons.

Pitons have one major fault. Although they do provide excellent protection, repeated placement and removal causes too much damage to rock walls. As soon as climbers realized that nuts were a good substitute for pitons—and, moreover, would not damage the cracks—the controversy over pitons and nuts began. To again use Bill Forrest's words:

> That the use of pitons was extravagant is evidenced by the violence with which they are currently being rejected. The pendulum has, in just a few years, swung from one extreme (driving pitons) to the other (placing nuts). Hopefully, the pendulum will soon come to rest in a position that accommodates common sense. It is unwise for a climber to complete an all-nut ascent that has incredibly bad belay anchors. Fixed pins are quite acceptable when natural and nut protection is not available. Praising all-nut ascents that had inadequate anchors fosters more than snobbery, it invites disaster. There are situations that require either hammer driven protection or retreat.

Chouinard's further advancement of climbing nuts was to redesign the common hexagonal nut. By elongating the lower tapers and by tapering both sides, he produced a nut with a possibility of four separate placements in four differently sized cracks. These nuts, known as Hexentrics, provided protection unheard of previously.

In Seneca Rocks, West Virginia, it was found that the Chouinard nuts were not suitable to the shape of the

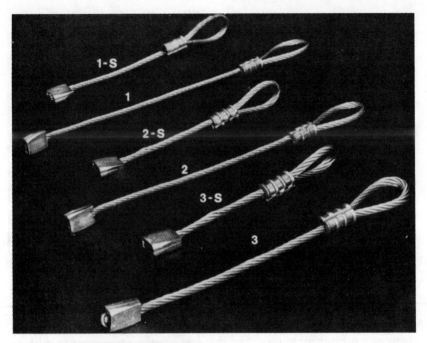

Forrest Arrowhead Nuts.
(Courtesy of Forrest
Mountaineering.)

Arrowhead Statistics

Nut Number	Top Width of Head	Head Height	Overall Length	Weight in oz.	Cable Diameter	Approximate Strength in lbs.
1	.238"	.663"	9-1/2"	1	1/8"	1,800
1-S	.238"	.663"	5-3/4"	1	1/8"	1,800
2	.295"	.732"	9-1/2"	1.5	5/32"	2,300
2-S	.295"	.732"	5-3/4"	1.5	5/32"	2,300
3	.400"	.875"	9-1/2"	2.5	3/16"	3,000
3-S	.400"	.875"	5-3/4"	2.5	3/16"	3,000

cracks peculiar to that area. A local climbing shop, the Gendarme, started to manufacture from standard bar stock their own version of a wedge nut, with a little wider taper, much more like the MOAC nut. These were christened Steven Stones and sold by the Gendarme.

Another new development came from Bill Forrest of Forrest Mountaineering. His nuts, called Copperheads, consist of a copper swage on the end of a cable. The copper is malleable, and when put into a crack, or even a tiny hole in the rock, and pounded with a hammer, they form to the shape of the crack or hole and remain in place. The more descriptive nickname, "bashies," has been adopted for these unique devices.

Choosing and Using Climbing Nuts

The technical rock climber of today is faced with a dilemma. Each designer and manufacturer of climbing nuts feels that his are the best and of the most advanced design. And he may be right. All nuts available in America today work really well. There are no inferior nuts on the market. So which to choose?

The best advice we can give is don't limit yourself to one manufacturer's model. Variety in your rack is most important. Different kinds of nuts can be used for different kinds of cracks and climbing situations. There is no nut that is perfect for all situations. Include a few Titons, some wedge Stoppers, some Hexentrics, etc. With a diverse rack, the protection possibilities are uncountable. Practice placing the various kinds you use to learn their holding strengths and limitations. Experiment with various combinations of nuts.

Deciding how many nuts to include on your rack is important. Nuts are directional anchors. They hold only in the direction in which they are jammed into the wall. A downward-slotted nut will hold a downward fall. An upward-slotted nut will hold an upward pull. A nut placed against another nut will jam into itself and therefore fill the gap of a larger crack, providing excellent protection. Nuts should be placed with more frequency than pitons. The harder the climb, the greater the number of nuts that should be placed. When establishing a belay, use a generous quantity of nuts. On an unfamiliar climb, carry even more nuts than are recommended in the guide book. It can't hurt to have a few extras.

Know your nuts. Color code each nut with a different cord or webbing. Then at a glance you can tell what nut you're reaching for. Once you've become familiar with the rack of equipment you're using, you'll always know that the red sling is a number six Stopper, the orange sling is a number eight Hexentric, the blue sling connects you to a number four Titon, and so on.

I've found from personal experience that putting cable nuts on one or two separate carabiners with gates opening outward helps in choosing a cable nut. I've also found that larger nuts are best racked with one carabiner per nut.

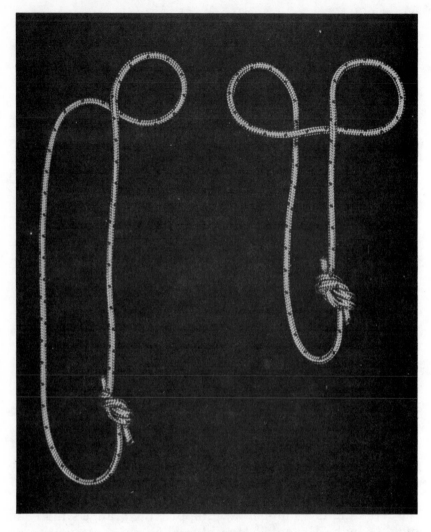

The sliding half hitch (also known as the munter hitch)
is a very useful knot in opposition placements as it provides
simple tension adjustment between nut placements,
and also ties off the 'biners it's connected to
thereby minimizing the force they could receive.
(Courtesy of Forrest Mountaineering.)

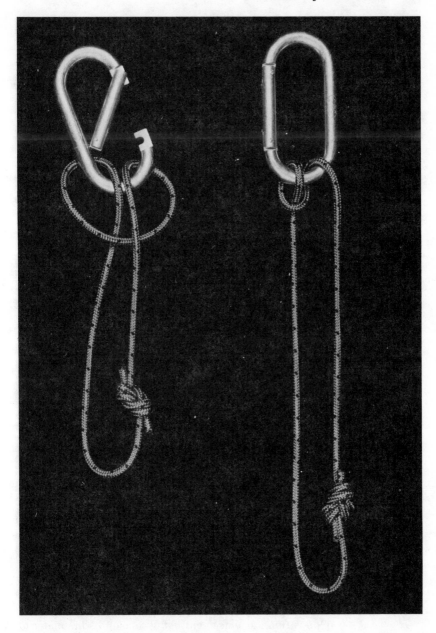

Opposition nut placement using rope and sling material.
(Courtesy of Forrest Mountaineering.)

This way, when you visually inspect a crack and mentally select the corresponding nut size, you don't have to worry about reaching down and looking for a carabiner. Just lift the nut off your climbing rack with the carabiner attached. Insert it into the crack, give it a tug for security, make sure it will stay in place, and clip in.

If you're using a new brand of nut for the first time, practice some test falls with it at a local boulder. If you're in doubt about the protection a nut may provide, talk about it with a climber who is already familiar with it.

Care and Maintenance

Nuts are almost indestructable and require very little care or maintenance. Most are made from aluminum alloys. Some are now anodized. If a nut becomes nicked or burred, it can be filed with a metal file.

The most critical thing about keeping nuts in ready condition is to change the sling material at least once a year if you climb frequently. If you don't use the nuts often enough to warrant changing the cordage every year, you should at least wash them in a mild soap to remove the grit and, if you use nonanodized nuts, aluminum oxide. If you have mechanical nuts, a spray of WD-40 into the moving parts will help remove dirt and dust and keep the parts freely moving.

If you're forced to use a hammer for the removal of a nut and the nut consequently becomes burred where the rope passes through, a smooth opening can be restored with a rat-tail file. If you're still using machine nuts, a rat-tail file will remove the inner threads. This is important in order to prevent your rope from being worn by passing over threads or burrs.

When I first strung my nuts I used flat, tubular tape. With the increase in the cost of nylon rope, it is again becoming a good idea to do this. One-inch tape may be used.

Cabled nuts tend, in time, to fray, especially the smaller

sizes. Watch for this, and when signs of fraying or wear become apparent, replace the nuts. If you replace old nuts with new models, save the old ones; they are excellent for practicing at the local crag areas.

Market Update

Chouinard Stoppers and Hexentrics are probably the most commonly used nuts. A great deal of thought and design have gone into them. I've used Chouinard nuts since they were first available in New England and am still thoroughly pleased with their excellent protection capability and versatility.

Chouinard Tube Chocks, which are becoming very hard to find, offer excellent protection in large cracks over 4 inches. If you are fortunate enough to locate them, they are a worthwhile investment.

Clogwyn Climbing Equipment has introduced an interesting variation of the Hexentric, called Clog Cogs. The Cogs have all the advantages of a standard hexagonal but are designed with a concave face. They are particularly well suited for stacking and for slotting into awkwardly sized cracks where a conventional hexagonal will not fit. Every Cog has five placement variations. They do look a little odd compared to what we are accustomed to, but with practice you will find them extremely useful and handy.

Besides the Copperheads mentioned earlier, Forrest Mountaineering manufactures nuts called Titons because of their T shape. These are their most versatile nuts; they provide both cam and jamming placements in a wide variety of cracks. In a vertical crack system, rotating the Titon lodges it in place. In a horizontal crack system, sideways placement results in an extremely secure running belay. In narrowing cracks, the Titon can successfully be slotted. This is one of the best nuts available for hard free-climbing.

Forrest also makes an aluminum wedge nut called the

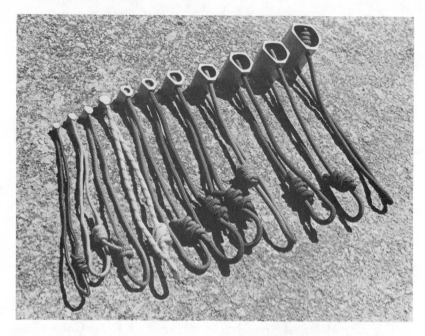

Chouinard Hexentrics.
(Courtesy of Great Pacific Iron Works.)

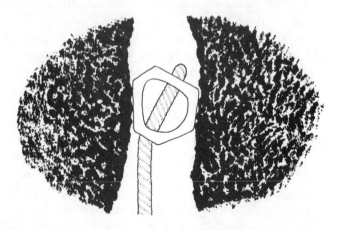

Above and opposite, the versatile Hexentric in use.
(Courtesy of Great Pacific Iron Works.)

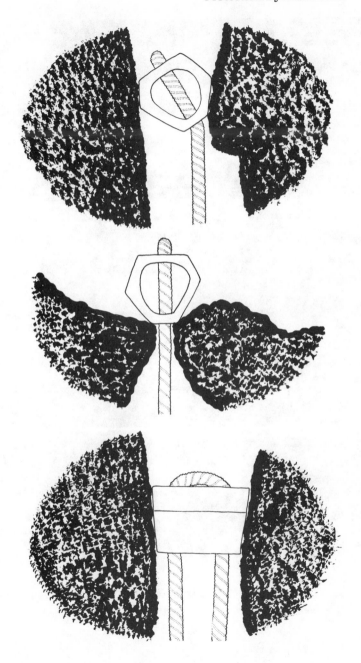

Tube Chocks.
(Courtesy of Great Pacific Iron Works.)

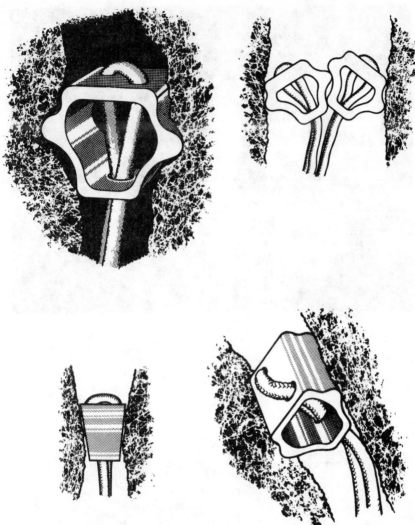

Clog Cogs in use.
(Courtesy of Climb High, Inc.)

Forrest Titons.
(Courtesy of Forrest Mountaineering.)

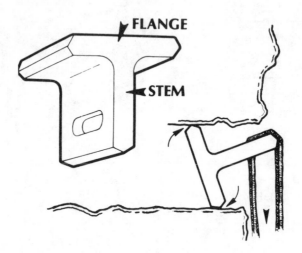

Foxhead. Since their introduction, Foxheads have established an outstanding record of usefulness and reliability.

One of the most radically different nuts, which has gained wide popularity in the United States, is Ray Jardine's Friend. The Friend, appropriately named, as you will find when you use it, is available in four sizes to fit cracks that vary in width from slightly over 1½ inches up to 5½ inches. Not since Lowe Alpine Systems designed their original spring-loaded climbing nuts have we seen anything as thoroughly in the realm of the technician as Friends. They are wonderful. They are adjusted to the size of the crack with a lever in the middle of the nut, which is pulled down to put tension on a wire cable connected to a flexible cam head. There are four movable cam heads per nut. These constrict downward with the pressure of the hand while pulling the plungerlike apparatus. When released, the cam heads grab into a crack. The ease of placement of the Friend is simply amazing. In parallel-sided cracks, they are the only protection device that one can use.

Jardine's Friends are referred to in climbing circles as "crack jumars." I was at first skeptical about them. When I used them, I backed them up with a conventional nut or well-driven piton. With use, and after a few falls, I came to appreciate their technical advantage and the advancement to climbing they represent. They are very expensive, ranging in price from twenty to forty dollars. An entire rack of conventional nuts can be had for the price of three Friends. If one were to carry a supply of ten to fourteen Friends, he would have made a substantial investment. However, if you can afford them, buy them. Serious climbers would probably consider them worth the investment.

Ed Leeper's newest contribution to the world of technical rock climbing is a radically new nut—again in a Z shape—made from the same material that his pitons are

*Placement of Titons, above, and Foxheads, right.
(Courtesy of Forrest Mountaineering.)*

made from. Most nuts are designed to fit into cracks and also to be used with a mechanical belaying device. Leeper Z nuts are designed to be used *without* a mechanical belaying device. An excessive load of energy placed upon the Leeper Z chock could result in a springlike action which would cause the Z nut not to hold as efficiently. The Z chock must be used in the narrow taper only, since its wide part does not offer the stability desirable in a properly placed nut. Since these nuts are so different from others, it is best to practice with them and to follow the manufacturer's suggestions and instructions carefully.

Nuts work with either a jamming or a camming action. For some situations, a conventional jamming chock is not

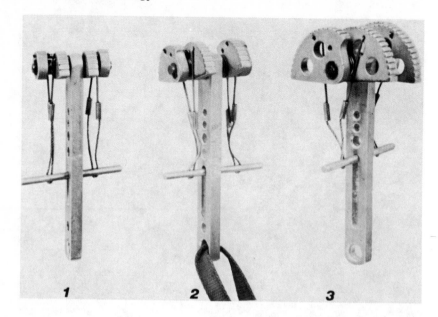

Ray Jardine's Friends,
sizes 1 through 3.
(Courtesy of ETS Claudius Simond et fils.)

as appropriate as a cam nut. Ed Leeper has devised a Cam Hook with numerous possibilities for use. Leeper says,

Clean climbing with a Cam Hook does not depend on irregularities of the crack. It uses nothing but the ordinary friction of steel on rock. Think of a climber in an extreme layback position. The leverage of his cantilevered body-weight provides the counter-pressure between his feet and hands that holds him in place.

Because the Cam Hook lever arm puts the eye at right angles from the flat bit of steel that goes in the crack, the pull on the eye can be from *any direction*. You can breathe and move around while standing on a Cam Hook. And with most placements, you can even lean back hard on it.

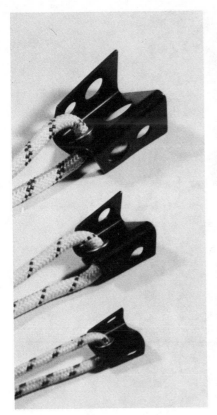

Leeper Z Chocks. (Courtesy of Ed Leeper.)

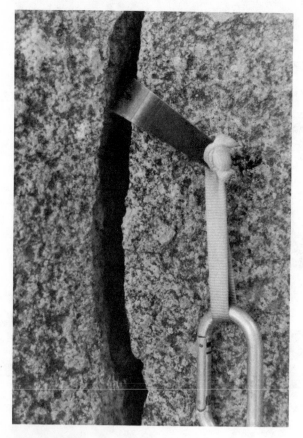

Leeper Cam Hook.
(Courtesy of Ed Leeper.)

Seattle Manufacturing Corporation (SMC) produces a good line of wedge Taper Locks and an excellent line of Camlock climbing nuts. I've used the Camlock nuts in narrow cracks, in flaring cracks, and in cracks that would be more resistant to other types of nuts. I've been pleased with them and always carry them on my aid rack.

The most diverse and complete line of climbing nuts is produced by Simond in France. They offer six varieties of nuts, each an independent design. They have their own version of a cabled wedge nut, an Asymetric Cable nut, an Asymetric nut on a sling, a wedge on a sling, a MultiCoins nut on a sling, a MultiCoins nut on cable, and—probably their most interesting and new design—a PolyCoins nut. The PolyCoins nut's most remarkable design feature is its stackability. Grooves are cut in each of the nuts to allow two or more nuts to be locked into place side by side in a crack. This greatly extends the range of protection possibilities. The MultiCoins is a cross between a wedge and a Hexentric and works similarly to the new Chouinard Hexentric in that it offers five possible protection arrangements. I've used the MultiCoins and found that it offers more protection than a wedge Stopper. It is not yet available in the United States, but I'm looking forward to its being imported in the near future.

The Troll company in England is the oldest manufacturer of climbing nuts. They manufacture a T-chock, a hexagonal chock, and a wedge. My favorite is the T-chock. They are hard to find in America, but if you do locate them, they are a good choice.

Campbell Mountaineering, Inc., is the latest American manufacturer to enter the market, with Campbell Saddlewedge chocks. These are all anodized, and each size is made in a different color, eliminating the need for the climber to color code his chocks. The Saddlewedge has grooved channels on the larger sides, which facilitate placement in irregular cracks.

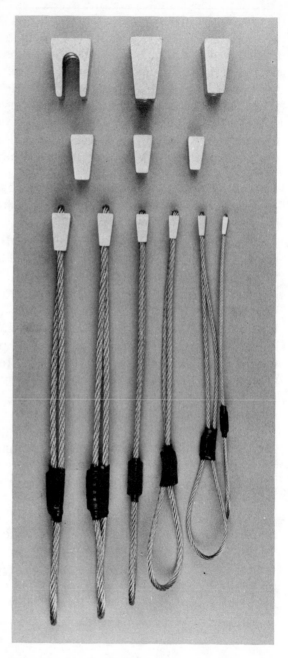

SMC Taperlocks and Camlocks.
(Courtesy of Seattle Manufacturing Corporation.)

Simond Cabled Wedge Nuts.
(Courtesy of ETS Claudius Simond et fils.)

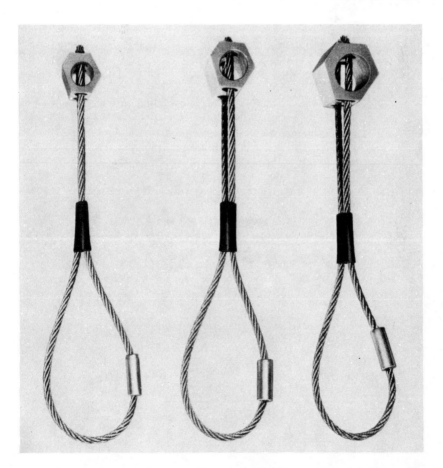

Simond Asymetric nuts on cable.
(Courtesy of ETS Claudius Simond et fils.)

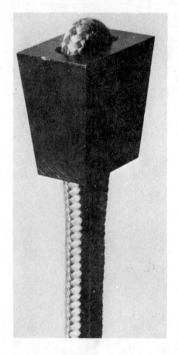

Left and below, *Simond wedge nuts and MultiCoins.*
(Courtesy of
ETS Claudius Simond et fils.)

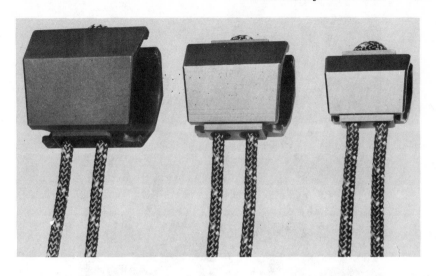

Above and below, Simond PolyCoins nuts.
(Courtesy of ETS Claudius Simond et fils.)

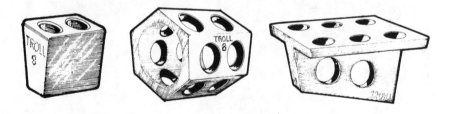

Troll nuts.
(Courtesy of Troll Safety Equipment, Ltd.)

3

Carabiners

A Little Background History

Climbers refer to carabiners by several different names: crabs, 'biners, snap-gates, or just plain carabiners. By whatever name, the mountaineering carabiner as we know it today is a relative newcomer to the climbing world. It evolved gradually over the years from the early 1900s in Europe when a climber would pass his rope through the eye of a piton in order to attach himself to the rock wall. Later, Alpine climbers realized that if they would attach a snap gate, used in building construction at that time, to the eye of a piton, it would ease attachment, and it would no longer be necessary to untie from the rope to pass it through the piton.

The steel shortage during World War II precipitated development of the aluminum carabiner. Early information about aluminum carabiners appeared in 1941 in *Appalachia Magazine* in an article by William P. House, a very active climber responsible for some of the difficult first ascents of major routes in the Shawangunks, on Cannon Cliff, and many rock outcroppings in the New England area. House was a member of the U.S. Army development committee for mountaineering equipment. The following text of his article gives an interesting glimpse into the origins of our modern carabiner, which we all take so much for granted. The original sketch of House's carabiner, which was submitted to the Development Division of the Aluminum Company of America, is also reprinted.

Some Preliminary Notes on Aluminum Carabiner

Few climbers who have felt the drag of three or four carabiner in their pockets or on their belts have not thought of the possibility of using a lighter metal. With this in view, the writer submitted samples of German and Swiss carabiner to the Development Division of the Aluminum Com-

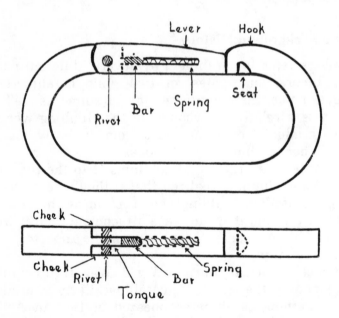

This original aluminum carabiner design submitted to the Aluminum Company of America appeared in the June 1941 issue of Appalachia.

pany of America, asking them to furnish an aluminum alloy duplicating as nearly as possible the strength qualities of the steel ones. They suggested an alloy S-T 24, in cross section $1/16$ of an inch greater than that of the sample, the rod being $3/8$ of an inch in diameter. This was furnished in heat-treated condition; but as it repeatedly broke on being bent, later material was annealed, and no further difficulty was experienced.

As might be imagined, duplicating as complicated an object as a carabiner without specially adapted machinery proved difficult. The amount of time spent was prodigious, but a skilled machinist at length turned out three good replicas. The most difficult step was fitting the coil spring and attached bar which provides the tension on the lever snap. Machining the lock head for the lever was also time-consuming, and some of the fits were not too tight. The completed parts were then heat-treated to restore stiffness, and the lever fastened to the hook by a steel rivet.

Dean Peabody kindly subjected these to breaking tests beside standard steel carabiner at his laboratory at M.I.T. The force was applied at opposite ends of the link gradually. The carabiner was considered "broken" when either the metal broke at the rivet, or a $3/8$ of an inch gap developed between the head of the lever and the hook. The results of Mr. Peabody's tests were as follows:

Steel	*Maximum Load (in lbs.)*	*Failure*
1	1,150	Lever slipped off seat at 500 lbs.; lever cleared seat projection at 1,100 lbs.; $3/8''$ gap at 1,150 lbs.
2	2,150	Tongue above rivet sheared out
Aluminum		
3	2,100	Lever cleared seat $3/8''$
4	2,040	Rivet sheared out at tongue; then lever slipped off seat
5	1,540	Rivet sheared out at tongue

These tests are not conclusive even for slow strains; but they do show the aluminum in a favorable light compared with the steel carabiner. Redesign of the tongue and groove at the base of the lever, allowing greater thickness to the tongue and slightly less to the cheeks, as well as placing the rivet farther from the top of the tongue, should add greatly to the strength of the carabiner. It might make the new aluminum ones stronger than the steel. Redesign of the seat so that pressure will lock the lever more tightly against the seat might also partially remedy the weakness of this part. Possibly making the seat slope inward slightly instead of having it horizontal would accomplish this. In any event, before any more strength tests are made, the weakness of the rivet section must be overcome.

If it proves possible to design the aluminum carabiner so that they are actually stronger than steel, the next step is to test for sudden strains, and then for strains at low temperatures. It is the opinion of some that aluminum will tend to crystallize at low temperatures and will not be able to withstand sudden jerks. Certainly this must be studied exhaustively before trust can be put in aluminum over steel.

Not enough work has yet been done to determine the probable cost of these carabiner produced in quantity. Even in normal times the cost of the intricate machines necessary to produce in quantity would be considerable. At the present time, with machine shop facilities at a premium, it does not appear as though they could be manufactured at much less than seventy-five cents, although this is a very hazardous estimate to make on the basis of the amount of work already done. Difficulties in getting the proper aluminum at this time may hold up progress; but the writer feels that the saving of approximately one-third in weight over the steel carabiner justifies going to considerable trouble to develop a dependable, light aluminum carabiner. The cooperation of others interested in this project will be greatly appreciated.

The result of House's work was that the U.S. government ordered thousands of aluminum carabiners to be manufactured. They were tested by the U.S. Army mountain troops stationed at Seneca Rocks, West Virginia. Raffi Bedayn, an officer of the mountain troops, further developed and modified the design, bringing its strength to over 2,000 pounds.

The carabiner has gone through many stages of development since then. All carabiners today operate on the simple principle of a lever that opens inward, allowing a rope to be attached. The carabiner should have a free-swinging gate that closes by itself, and a minimum test strength of 2,000 pounds. The UIAA has determined that a carabiner should hold a fall factor of two. Most carabiners manufactured today meet this standard. If you should happen to find one of the old military 'biners, it is suggested that you keep it as a souvenir only, since modern carabiners offer much greater safety.

Choosing and Using Carabiners

In choosing a carabiner, make sure that the ones you buy open under body-weight. I remember struggling with some of the 'biners I used when first doing aid climbs. I had a terrible experience hanging from one of the carabiners, unable to clip in the rope because the 'biner didn't open under body-weight. Almost all of the carabiners available today do open under body-weight.

Often, on a long climb, one comes across pitons fixed in the wall. When one tries to put in an offset D 'biner with a large eye, it is almost impossible to pass the hook end of the 'biner through. If this should happen, a small piece of nylon tape threaded through the eye of the piton, with the 'biner attached to it, facilitates clipping in. A cable nut passed through the eye of the piton can also be used to clip into the protection point. Always make sure your 'biner is hooked into the protection point with the gate opening downward and out from the wall so that if the carabiner should be pushed against the wall the gate will

not open. If the gate does open it will weaken the carabiner.

Carabiners come in oval shapes, D-shapes, a modified D,
offset, and with locking gates. Offset and D-shaped 'biners
are structurally stronger than ovals. The load of a fall is
transferred along the back of the offset and D, and away
from the gate opening, which is the weakest point of the
'biner, and the point of all 'biner failures.

A locking-gate carabiner has attached to its gate a
sheath of aluminum that screws down to close. This
prevents accidental opening of the gate by any amount of
pressure. To open the carabiner, one must turn the gate. In
situations where a rope might accidentally put pressure
on the outside of a carabiner, it is recommended that this
type be used. Locking carabiners should always be used in
rappelling and for belaying. When attaching a figure-of-
eight knot to any convenient belay tie-in, it is possible for

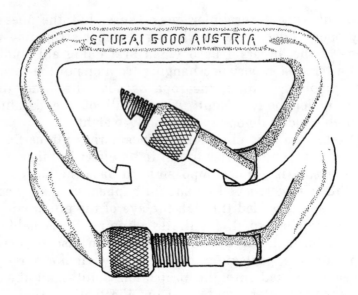

Locking-gate carabiner, open and closed.

that figure-of-eight to rotate on the 'biner and cross its gate, becoming unclipped. This is particularly true when using a clove-hitch knot for tying-in on a hanging belay. If a locking-gate carabiner is not available, two carabiners with opposite gates give the same effect.

Life expectancy of any carabiner is indefinite. They can be used for years provided they aren't damaged by a hammer blow or subjected to a severe leader-fall. A carabiner that has been dropped from a climb and found at the base of the cliff should be regarded with suspicion. Hairline fractures can develop in aluminum after a long fall. If you drop your own carabiner, don't rely on it any longer for safety. It is potentially weaker, therefore dangerous to use. If you find a 'biner, use it for cleaning purposes only.

In aid climbing, a retrieving carabiner—one that is attached to the piton and left attached when removing the peg with a hammer—should not be used as a protection 'biner.

Carabiners have been known to break, and pins that hold carabiners together have been known to slip out. You may return such a broken carabiner to the manufacturer. All manufacturers are interested in knowing how their 'biners are damaged and what actually causes them to fail. A reputable manufacturer will be glad to send you a replacement.

Occasionally, during a climb, after one has extended a running belay by attaching a sling and 'biner to it, the 'biner may run over the edge of the cliff on a sharp, right-angle projection. In the event of a fall it is very possible for the 'biner to be pushed against this right-angle projection and opened part-way when the fall is held. If this situation is obvious during the course of setting up the running belay, attaching the rope to a spare locking-gate carabiner can prevent the carabiner from opening and losing part of its strength.

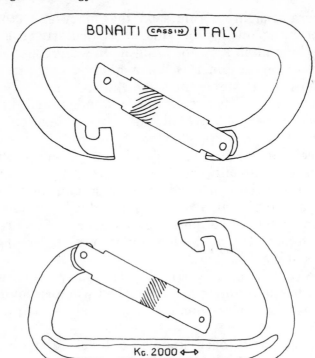

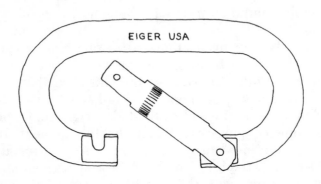

D, offset, and oval carabiners.

Care and Maintenance

Carabiners are available in plain aluminum or with an anodized coating. When using a nonanodized carabiner, you will notice that after constant use, the moisture and salts from your hands and body will oxidize the surface of the carabiner. This oxidization can be removed with a mild soap or detergent. Spraying WD-40 or a silicone penetrating lubricant in the spring gate after it has been cleaned will help. I have recently replaced all of my old 'biners with new anodized models because, after a long climb, my face and hands were almost black from the aluminum oxide. The United States Food and Drug Administration has recently completed an investigation of early deaths among employees in aluminum plants that showed a high percentage of aluminum particles accumulated in their brains. I don't mean to be an alarmist, but the new anodized carabiners are certainly cleaner and, in the long run, perhaps safer.

Market Update

Following is a selection of the best carabiners on the U.S. market.

The Clog carabiner is available in oval, offset, and D shapes—both anodized and nonanodized. My personal climbing rack consists of all Clog 'biners. I have found that they are the best designed and easiest to use of any carabiner available today. The latch has been redesigned recently, with a much greater angle. This advantage can be critical when clipping into a bent piton on those hard 5.10s. The Clog 'biner that I use is the 10 millimeter offset anodized model. Its breaking strength is 4,600 pounds; its weight is 55 grams. I've been using Clogs for the last six years and am completely satisfied with their performance on the wall and their handling characteristics in winter climbing.

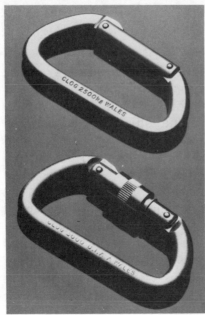

Above and left, *Clog carabiners.*
(Courtesy of
Climb High, Inc.)

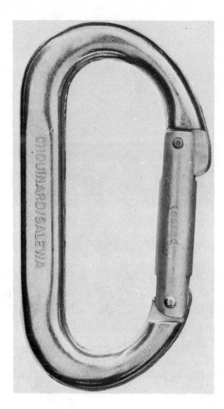

Chouinard carabiner.
(Courtesy of
Great Pacific Iron Works.)

New innovations in carabiners were made by the Salewa Company in Germany. They developed the hollow carabiner, first introduced in the United States by the Great Pacific Iron Works. This carabiner is extremely light in weight and made from hollow tubular aluminum rather than from bent bar stock or forged aluminum, which makes it considerably lighter, yet very strong. If one needs to carry 30 or 40 'biners for a long aid climb, this is a definite advantage.

The Chouinard carabiner from the Great Pacific Iron Works has been popular on big-wall racks since its introduction in 1957. The new modified-D Chouinard carabiner combines the simplicity of the oval with the strength of

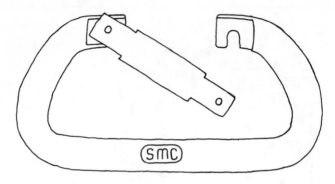

SMC carabiner.

the D. Stainless steel gate rivets are manufactured for reliability and extra strength for side loads. The test strength of this modified D is 2,200 kilograms and it weighs 2.4 ounces.

The Chouinard oval 'biner is perhaps the strongest oval available. Its simplicity makes it easy to handle. One can always tell which way the gate opens by feeling the latch, which is slightly larger than the pivot point. The test strength is over 2,200 kilograms; it weighs 2.4 ounces.

Seattle Manufacturing Corporation (SMC) carabiners are made from high-strength aluminum alloy with stainless steel interior parts. They come in ovals and D shapes. Both open under body-weight and will accept an 11 millimeter rope with two étriers clipped in. SMC also makes a locking-gate carabiner. The SMC standard oval is an excellent choice. A small bump on the gate side of the oval helps the climber locate the opening.

The Simond Company of Chamonix, France, has been producing carabiners for the past ten years. They offer 'biners of both steel and aluminum. Their locking-gate carabiners come in a variety of designs, from offset with flat body profile to round with tubular locking-gates. I've

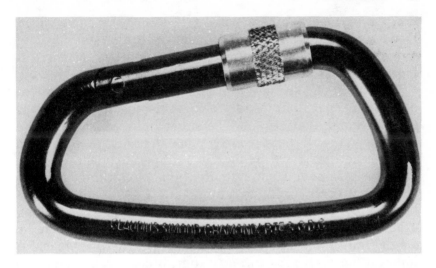

Simond locking-gate carabiner.
(Courtesy of
ETS Claudius Simond et fils.)

used Simond carabiners in the winter and have found that their offset locking model handles extremely well and does not ice up.

Bonaiti carabiners, manufactured in Italy and distributed in the United States by Liberty Mountain Sports, are available in locking D, oval, locking oval, and offset ultra-light. The Bonaiti 'biner has been around in the United States for over ten years and is an old favorite of climbers. I've used all of the Bonaiti models. The one I prefer is the ultra-light; it's easy to clip into bent pitons and, because of its small size, it keeps the weight down when you carry a lot of 'biners.

Liberty Mountain Sports manufactures and distributes its own brand of carabiners. The Liberty 'biner is available in oval and locking D. The ovals are anodized. They are available in red, blue, and orange. Liberty also produces an ultra-light 'biner, lighter even than the Bonaiti.

Early Liberty carabiners were sold under the name Eiger. However, these were definitely not up to the standards of today's Liberty 'biner, which was developed after correcting the defects of the Eiger.

The Robbins/Salewa hollow tube carabiner is exceptionally strong, yet light. Made to Robbins specifications, it is of traditional oval design. The super light weighs only 1½ ounces, yet will hold nearly 4,000 pounds. A minimum test strength of 1,100 pounds is stamped by hand on each carabiner. Believe it or not, Robbins Mountaingear actually tests each of its carabiners to 2,500 pounds. This testing, by the way, does not weaken them. The testing assures not only no bad batches of carabiners, but also no single faulty ones. With the lesser weight of this carabiner, a big wall rack of sixty-four 'biners would be up to 4 pounds lighter. For a situation where light weight is essential and yet strength is necessary, the super light, Robbins hollow carabiner is highly recommended.

The LaPrade/Desmaison carabiner offers extreme strength in its standard D model. It has a blind gate for protection from the rock, and uses stainless steel rivets and springs in construction. The strength is 2,800 kilograms; it weighs 2.4 ounces. Another model of the LaPrade/Desmaison 'biner is a 2,200 kilogram model, also in a D shape, with a highly polished finish, which weighs 2 ounces. These are manufactured in France and distributed in the United States by Robbins Mountain Gear.

4

Harnesses

A Little Background History

The climbing harness developed naturally out of a need for safety, comfort, and freedom, but more importantly, from the need for a longer rope. Prior to the twentieth century, the method of tying into a climbing rope was to pass several loops of the rope around the waist and tie-in with a knot. This method, however, easily used up about 15 feet of the rope just for tying in. If both the lead climber and his second tied into the same rope, their 150-foot rope ended up only 120 feet long. Thus, their climbing was restricted to those routes having less than 120 feet between belay points or secure stance locations.

British climbers solved this problem by taking a short section of hemp rope and wrapping it around their waists. They tied this section of rope, which was wrapped a minimum of four times around the waist, with a secure knot, then tied directly into this section of rope with the end of the climbing line. This gave both climbers maximum use of their 150-foot rope.

During World War II, with a shortage of hemp, manufacturers began to use nylon for climbing ropes, and flat webbing. The flat webbing, a little more than 1-inch wide, was found to be a suitable substitute for a conventional rope harness. In some sections of the country, climbers still tie-in this way.

The problem with this kind of tie-in system is that the shock load from a fall is transmitted directly to the spinal area. A rope sling or tape (flat-webbing) sling wrapped around the waist also tends to ride up underneath the climber's rib cage. In the event of a fall, ribs are easily broken. Some good climbers do use this type of rope sling, but for safety purposes it is not recommended.

The next step in the evolution of today's harness was the use of 1-inch tape or flat nylon webbing as a rappel seat. The rappel seat was constructed by taking about a ten-foot section of flat tape and tying it securely. This knot and its tie-in created a large loop. The loop was passed under the buttocks and around the back. By reaching down between the legs, one of the strands of the rope was drawn up. Thus, loops of rope came around the right and left sides of the back and one came up between the legs. The loops, when connected with a carabiner, formed a very convenient and comfortable rappel seat. The U.S. Army mountain troops during World War II used this for rappelling. It was an effective way of taking pressure off the legs and back. However, there was still some discomfort because the clip-in point was very low on the body, almost at the genital area. Climbers then discovered that if two loops were made in the webbing, when they were suspended, the back of the legs would take pressure off the climber during a rappel.

The earliest harness I remember seeing was made of 1-inch tape. This consisted of a 20- or 25-foot piece of 1-inch webbing with leg loops to the right and left of the middle. The loops were large enough for the legs to slip into easily but not so large that the loops would fall down the legs. The remaining webbing was wrapped around the body and secured with a water knot. A locking-gate carabiner was hooked through the webbing between the two knots and the crotch, and into the webbing that passed around the back and chest. This is still one of the most inexpensive ways of constructing a safe and comfortable harness. It is easy to construct, and the cost is under ten dollars.

For rappelling with this harness one could take another small section of rope, clip it into a locking-gate carabiner, and into a 'biner on the wall, allowing the freedom to set up a rappel.

About 1967, the Trailwise Company began producing a harness that fit around the back and was secured with 1-inch webbing. It was 4 inches wide and made of standard seat-belt webbing. This harness had a separate pair of leg loops of 2-inch seat-belt webbing, which produced two leg-loops and a tie-in point for connecting the harness around the back and stomach to the leg loops. This was the first two-piece harness that I remember seeing in the United States. It was widely used in the Northeast. Local harness makers copied it, and soon many manufacturers were producing harnesses of a similar design.

Another major reason for development of the harness was the interest in big-wall climbing in Yosemite Valley. It was found that tying into a rope was not suitable, and that a harness which could suspend the body from the back of the thighs and the buttocks was essential.

Choosing and Using a Harness

There are many harnesses now available in the United States. The two most popular are the Forrest Mountaineering waist- and leg-loop combination seen in climbing areas in the West, and the Whillans Sit Harness, designed by Don Whillans for the British Annapurna Expedition in 1970. Other types of harnesses include the Swami Belt, a rope tie-in harness, the waist and leg loop combination (referred to as the seat harness), and a harness more popular in Europe which combines the leg and waist loop with a chest harness.

The chest harness is made of rope or flat webbing and is wrapped around the climber's chest. Two pieces of rope come up and around the climber's back and over his shoulder. This chest harness is secured by tying directly in at the points on the chest. This harness has proven to be very dangerous when used alone. Although it supports the climber in a much more upright position than waist- and leg-loop harnesses, when not used in conjunction with a waist and leg loop tie-in, it is possible for the climber's arms to be raised directly above his head by a fall and for the entire unit to slip over his head. This has happened. The chest harness also puts too much pressure underneath the arms. If the harness should slide up, it could cut off circulation, leaving the climber suspended and unable to use his hands.

If a climber should fall from an overhang into a free-hanging position, he might be unable to reconnect with the wall. It has been shown that if he is wearing a Swami Belt and is unable to relieve its pressure on his stomach and backbone, he could actually suffocate in as little as twenty minutes. The pressure put on the rib cage and lungs is tremendous.

If you doubt this you might want to test it by suspending yourself a few feet above the ground from a tree (with a friend nearby for safety) to see how long you can hang. Of course, more than likely, you will ease your body into a nice comfortable position, so this won't convince you. A better test would be to set up a ladder and take a fall of about 6 feet. Let the rope impact be transmitted to your body. Then try the same thing using a harness with leg loops. I'm sure you will agree that a harness with leg loops is much more comfortable, and much safer.

A body harness supports the body under the legs, around the back, and over the shoulders. It distributes the shock of a fall evenly over the body. Because of its unique design, it holds a climber in an upright position during a fall. A body harness also facilitates evacuation from crevasses and is comfortable when artificial climbing or climbing over roofs. It is the safest harness of all.

Tying In

There are as many methods of tying into a harness as there are harness manufacturers. It has been found that the safest way is to tie the rope directly to the harness. Most manufacturers recommend this procedure. We do not recommend that climbers secure the harness to a locking-gate carabiner and then to the rope. With this method, there are three possible points of failure: the carabiner, the rope, and the harness. Carabiners have been known to fail; ropes have not; they don't break. So, when tying into whatever harness you're using, tie in with a rope.

There are times when clipping into the harness with a carabiner is justifiable, if it is impossible to use a rope. This can happen when you're the middle man on the rope. In these cases a figure-of-eight knot on a bight of rope secured with a locking-gate carabiner would be safe and reasonable. The strongest locking-gate carabiner that the climber has should be used. We highly recommend the Clog 13 millimeter, UIAA-approved, locking offset 'biner, although any other locking 'biner would be sufficient.

Care and Maintenance

All harnesses today are made from either nylon tape or

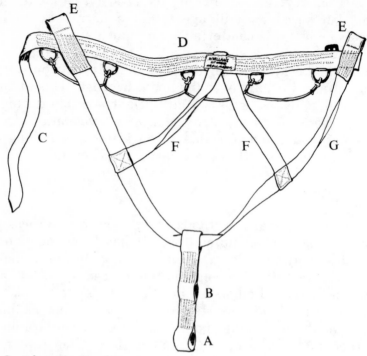

A: Crutchstrap—Top loop
B: Crutchstrap—Twin loop
   for carabiner
C: Waist strap
D: Waist belt
E: Tie in loops
F: Buttock strap
G: Thigh strap

Above and right, *Proper tie-in with*
Whillans harness.
(Courtesy of Troll Safety Equipment, Ltd.)

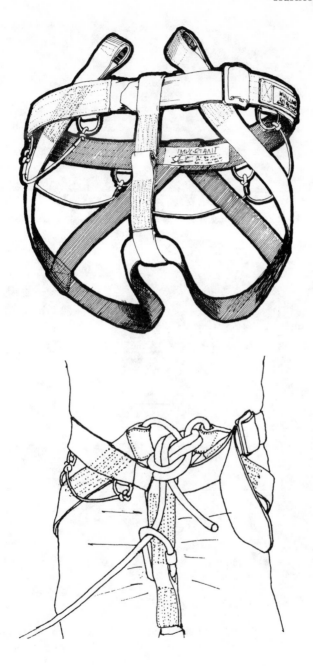

Above and right, Simond "Super Pro" body harness.
(Courtesy of ETS Claudius Simond et fils.)

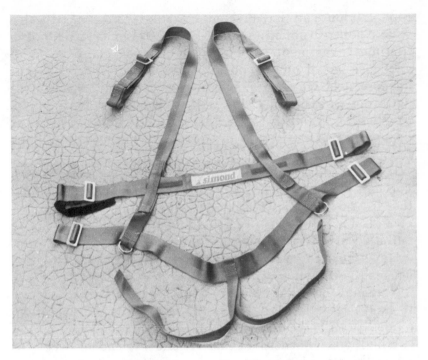

rope. Nylon can be affected by solar radiation. It also wears when rubbed against rock. A harness is not a lifetime investment, though you can get many years of good use out of one if you take care of it properly. If your harness gets very dirty, wash it on gentle cycle in a non-agitating washing machine with Ivory Snow, New Dawn, or Woolite. Wash in cold water and do not use bleach or heavy detergent. If you air-dry your harness it will be flexible and as good as new.

If the webbing of your harness should become frayed, you can reseal it by heating a knife and holding it against the frayed section. The hot knife will melt the frayed strands back together. While doing this, be careful not to cut any part of the harness, or yourself.

Never mark your harness with Magic Marker; this causes a weakening of the nylon.

You may notice a black residue on your harness where it has been attached to carabiners. This is aluminum oxide; it can be easily washed off.

When your harness begins to show signs of wear, or when the stitching begins to pull apart, it is time to buy a new one.

Market Update

Simond Equipment produces two full body harnesses. The "Super Pro" model is the best. It is adjustable at the waist, hips, and shoulders. Tie-in is done at six separate points, all meeting at the waist. Recommended knots for tying in are the double bowline and the figure-of-eight. The "Super Pro" is made from 2-inch nylon tape sewn across the back of the shoulders to prevent any movement of the shoulder straps. The leg loops are adjustable for size, a nice feature for climbing in heavy pile pants.

The Simond "Super Pro" harness is the top of the line of French harnesses, and for those who require a full-body harness, we give it our full endorsement.

The other recommended Simond harness is the "Artif," another full body harness with the same adjustability features as the "Super Pro." The chest section can be used as the direct tie-in, or you can tie into the waist area. It is a little awkward to tie into both chest and waist, as this requires a large loop of rope. The manufacturer recommends that when tying in directly, you tie into the waist loops then pass the rope through a locking-gate carabiner at the chest level. In case of a serious fall, the climber will be suspended in a full vertical position. In glacial climbing, where a separate tie-in might be necessary, a rope could be attached directly to the harness at the chest level. The "Artif" is a versatile harness, extremely comfortable in the leg area, with separate adjustments on the back.

Simond harnesses unfortunately are not sold in the United States; they must be ordered directly from the manufacturer in France.

There are several Millet rock-climbing harnesses. The three we like are the Walter Bonatti, model 740; the Batard Complete, model 780; and the Millet model 777.

The Bonatti harness is a conventional seat harness with a single tie-in in the front. It's very similar to most of the European body-harnesses on the American market. However, it is adjustable at the waist, which is a great benefit when adding or subtracting layers of clothes.

The Bonatti is made from 1-inch and 16 millimeter nylon webbing. Shoulder straps are adjustable, as are thigh straps. The thigh straps do not have buckles for adjustment; the adjustment is done by sliding buttock-straps that pull the thigh strap snug.

When untying from this harness in a rappel situation, it is necessary first to secure both of the front loops with a locking-gate carabiner so the harness won't fall off.

The Batard Complete harness features a seamless chest, back adjustment for the webbing, and adjustments for thigh, waist, and shoulder fit. It is our favorite of the

This page and opposite,
Simond "Artif" harness.
(Courtesy of
ETS Claudius Simond et fils.)

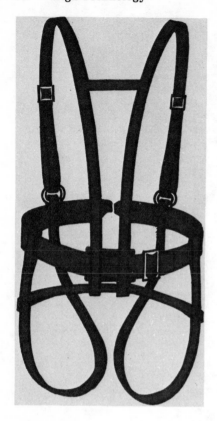

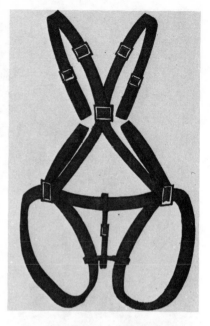

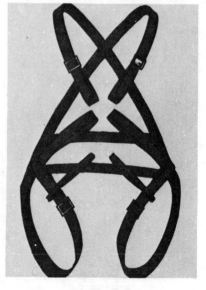

*Millet harnesses. Above,
Walter Bonatti, model 740;
above right, Batard Complete,
model 780; right, model 777.
(Courtesy of Sacs Millet, S.A.)*

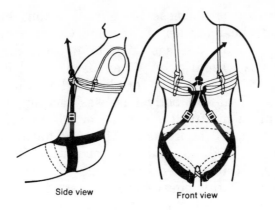

Side view   Front view

Edelrid seat and chest harnesses.
(Courtesy of Liberty Mountain Sports.)

Millet harnesses. It's a new harness, introduced this past year. As is true of all Millet harnesses, breaking strength is at 4,400 pounds, or two tons. That's pretty strong.

The Millet model 777 is a standard-size body harness, featuring a tie-in for legs, waist, and chest. The harness was designed to be used by guided parties and climbing schools, and is the least expensive of the three.

The Edelrid seat harness when used in conjunction with the Edelrid chest harness is the equivalent of a safe and comfortable body harness. We do not recommend that either be used separately. When used together and tied with a figure-of-eight knot or double bowline, they provide an excellent full body harness. Lacking in this harness is a place to attach a hammer or additional accessory cords for hanging equipment. The seat harness is available in small, medium, and large sizes; the chest harness fits chests of 80 to 110 centimeters.

The Edelrid Badile chest harness, made from 45 millimeter webbing, is fully adjustable at both the shoulder points and in the back with a double sliding-buckle system. Two large rings on the chest harness allow contact points for equipment.

The Edelrid Futura full body harness has adjustable shoulder, back, and leg loops. It is made from 45 millimeter perlon tape. One does not have to step through the leg loops to put this on. The Futura keeps the body upright during a fall. There are hammer holster-attachments on each side of the harness.

I first became acquainted with Clan Robertson harnesses in 1974 when a friend showed me one of the original models. At that time they were manufactured by the Colorado Alpine School and sold under the Clan Robertson label. It was then possible to buy Clan Robertsons around the Boulder, Colorado, area, but they later disappeared from the American market, at least in the East. I am pleased that they have reappeared.

There are two excellent Clan Robertson seat harnesses, the best of which is the Pro Harness. This is an all-purpose harness, designed for big-wall and artificial climbing. It features a 3-inch waist belt, a hauling line loop, a belay anchor section, accessory equipment cords, and fully adjustable leg straps. You tie in by passing the rope around the 3-inch belt and through a tie-in loop produced by the leg loops. Secured with a figure-of-eight

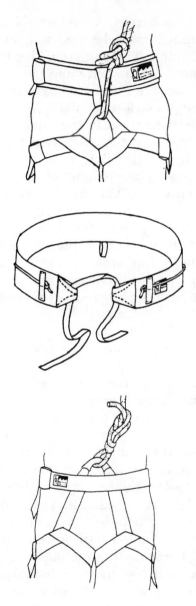

*Clan Robertson harnesses. Top,
Pro Harness; center, Mountain
Belt; bottom, Guide Harness.
(Courtesy of Robbins
Mountaingear.)*

knot and double bowline, this harness is extremely comfortable and useful for rappelling, belaying, and, as we mentioned, for big-wall climbing. The adjustable leg loops are one of its best features. It is extremely well put together and is one of the top five harnesses available. It is made in extra-small through extra-large sizes.

The second Clan Robertson harness is the Guide Harness. Its best feature is its low price. One size fits all. Buckles on the waist and leg loops allow it to be easily adjusted to almost any size. This is one of the best harnesses to use in instructional situations. It's an inexpensive protection harness specifically designed for students and clubs and is especially good for organizations which need one harness that will fit people of varying sizes. It has cross-connected adjustable leg loops and is very high-waisted to ensure that the wearer will not be suspended upside down. It has a direct tie-in of reinforced material.

Clan Robertson also produces a Swami Belt. When used in conjunction with the Clan Robertson leg loops it forms a very comfortable, one-system seat harness.

Forrest Mountaineering's Swami Belt and leg-loop belt was introduced in 1968 and became immediately popular in climbing circles for its comfort and convenience. It is a very simple system. It provides a secure and comfortable seat for rappels, hanging belays, jumars, pendulums, and is excellent for free climbing. It was designed to distribute the impact force of a fall to the thighs and the waist. It comes in 2- and 3-inch models. The Swami Belt is made of a single piece of nylon webbing. It tapers in the front for an easy tie-in. It is tied to the climber with a 5-foot piece of 1-inch tubular webbing. There is an attachment loop of sewn webbing on the back, which allows the leg loops to be attached, preventing them from sliding down. The leg loops are constructed from nylon webbing of 2- and 3-inch widths.

To secure the front webbing to the harness, you pass the 1-inch webbing through both loops of the Swami Belt. It is tied tightly around the waist, using a ring bend or water knot. The manufacturer strongly recommends that when tying this knot at least a 2½-inch piece of webbing be exposed at the end of the knot. The rope is then tied around the 1-inch webbing and through the leg-loop attachment. Secure the Swami Belt and leg loops together with either a figure-of-eight or a double bowline. Pass the adjustment strap on the back of the leg loops through the loop in the back of the harness. With this you can adjust the tension for the leg loops. You can wear it loosely for free climbing or a little bit more snugly for aid climbing.

The basic design of the Forrest Swami Belt has not changed greatly since 1968. The fact that it has survived twelve years and is still being manufactured is an indication of a good harness. We have used this Forrest combination ourselves. The only modification we made was to have a cobbler permanently attach a hammer holster to the harness. Forrest Mountaineering says, "Do not attach the climbing rope to the Forrest harness with a carabiner as this adds unnecessary risk to the system." We recommend that every harness be tied directly into the rope; do not use a carabiner.

Forrest Mountaineering is probably the best purveyor of big-wall climbing equipment in America. This harness has been used on many big walls. It is comfortable, and one of the top five models we recommend.

The Edelweiss sit harness is manufactured by one of the best rope manufacturers in the world. It has no buckles, which makes it a very lightweight harness. Without these buckles, however, the harness must be purchased to fit the exact size of the person using it. Extremely thick webbing is used to dissipate a shock load. Attachment to the harness is provided by four loops, two at the waist and two below the waist. The rope is tied in with an upward

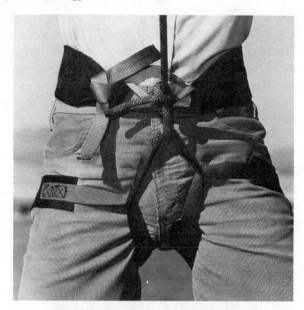

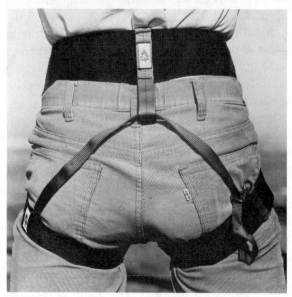

Forrest Swami Belt and leg loops.
(Courtesy of Forrest Mountaineering.)

motion, the rope having been passed down through the first loop of webbing and up through the webbing on the other side. To prevent the harness from becoming detached from the climber when untied from the rope, a separate piece of webbing is provided to secure all four loops. All four loops are attached by the 1-inch webbing and secured with a ring bend or water knot. Again, it is recommended that a 2½-inch tail of rope be left on both sides of the knot. Besides being one of the lightest harnesses you can use, the Edelweiss is economical. It is available in sizes small, medium, and large, from waist size 26 through 40.

We've had the opportunity to meet and talk with people from Troll Equipment on several occasions over the past few years. We feel that their products reflect the highest standards of quality and design.

Perhaps the best harness for a variety of climbs in the United States is the Troll-Whillans sit harness. This is a very versatile, multipurpose harness. Developed by Don Whillans and Troll Equipment for use in free and artificial climbing, belaying, rappelling, and caving, it is constructed of 50 millimeter nylon tape. The minimum breaking strength is in excess of 2,000 kilograms. It is a lightweight harness, using a buckle system with a slippage testing strength of over 4,000 pounds. Built into the harness is an attachment point for a locking-gate carabiner. Sewn directly to the harness is a series of rings tied together with nylon parachute cord. The parachute cord greatly aids hanging and racking of your equipment.

I have personally taken a 40-foot leader fall in the Whillans harness and landed upright. The harness absorbed most of the shock. We have used only the Troll-Whillans sit harness in all of our climbing programs for the past four years. We have found, though, that there are some people whom the Whillans sit harness will not fit. You should try it on before buying. If it rides too high over the hip bone, or if, when you suspend yourself from a

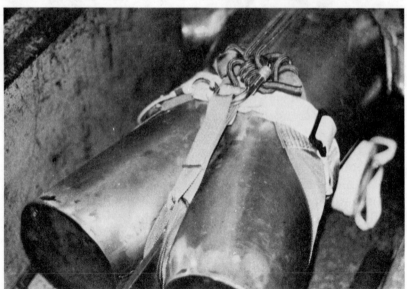

Testing Troll harnesses at the manufacturers.
(Courtesy of Troll Safety Equipment, Ltd.)

rope, it digs too much into your stomach, it might be that you need another harness. But if you do buy a Whillans, you are buying one of the best.

The Troll body harness is the best available today. It is easy to adjust; you can add or remove extra clothing while wearing it by simply releasing the buckle system, slipping on or off a vest or parka, and retightening the buckle. With the Troll harness, you can choose either chest or waist attachments for ropes. It is the safest harness I know of; there is absolutely no possibility of the wearer flipping over during a fall while wearing the Troll body harness.

If you would like to make your own harness, there is a kit for this purpose manufactured by Mountain Safety Research. They have recently discontinued the kit, but it should be available in mountaineering shops for awhile yet. Be sure to follow the harness construction directions to the letter, and be sure to use the thread that MSR provides. We strongly urge that you don't try to make a harness without using a kit; don't even have a cobbler make one for you. If cotton thread were used, it might rot, or the stitches might weaken and break.

5

Helmets

To Wear or Not to Wear

Almost everyone realizes by now that it makes good sense to wear a helmet while riding a motorcycle, in order to prevent a serious head injury. In fact, most states now require this by law. Strangely, the same good sense does not carry over to those who climb mountains. There are still climbers who feel it shows signs of being a novice to don a helmet before climbing. Climbing *does* have dangers, and one of them is the very real possibility of being hit on the head, either by a falling rock or a falling piece of equipment from another climber. It is the nature of rock walls—except for those wonderful, solid granite walls of Yosemite—to have loose fragments and pieces due to natural weathering—freezing and thawing over the years. This loose rock falls. Even earthbound motorists are familiar with the "Caution, Falling Rock" signs that decorate our highways. One of these falling missiles could be headed directly for your skull.

A helmet, particularly one with an inner suspension system, will deflect and distribute the shock from a blow over the entire head. A good helmet will absorb a great deal of the shock. I have seen people whose helmets were struck by quite large objects while they were wearing them. The helmets broke, but all the climbers received were shocks.

Every year the American Alpine Club publishes a report called *Accidents in American Mountaineering.* On the average, there are five incidents reported each year of head injuries that could have been avoided by wearing a helmet.

In 1973 I was involved in the removal of two climbers from Cannon Cliff in New Hampshire. The head of one of the climbers had repeatedly banged against the rock during the course of his fall. Not to go into detail, but it was, to say the least, an unpleasant sight that greeted his rescuers. Neither of the climbers survived. Neither was wearing a helmet or harness; either of these safety devices might have saved them.

Of course, there are no rules about wearing helmets. It is still a matter of personal choice. And, since climbing is one of the few remaining sports unencumbered by excessive rules and regulations, appealing to free-spirited people, it is not suggested that any rules of this nature be applied. However, it does seem to me that every conscientious and sensible climber would consider a good, strong helmet a most necessary part of his climbing gear.

A Little Background History

When I began climbing in New Hampshire over ten years ago, not very many climbers wore helmets—for different reasons than today: they were not easily available in those days. Those that were seen were usually the inside liners of World War II combat helmets, painted by climbers in a variety of colors. Some climbers wore military surplus, leather flying caps—bizarre-looking things with head bands that hung down below the ears. The flying caps were not really good protection for climbing; they would have been better for boxing. But they were better than no helmet at all. Later, climbers seeking head protection wore kayaking helmets or the Bell helmet, which became popular in the 1960s as *the* climbing hat.

The use of helmets in mountaineering began where so much of mountaineering did, in Europe. Earlier climbers there wore wide-brimmed hats, primarily to shield their eyes from the glare of the strong sun in the Alpine snow and ice fields. They discovered that these wide-brimmed hats also offered protection from falling pebbles.

Eventually, the hard helmet was developed in Europe, but it took awhile before it made its debut in America. However, as climbing became more and more popular in the United States, the support industry of manufacturers and distributors of climbing equipment grew, and climbing helmets began to appear in greater numbers out West and in the Eastern climbing areas.

The first helmets used in America were those brought by climbers who had been overseas. One of the early helmets I encountered was a Galibier rock-climbing helmet—a very thin plastic shell with an internal suspension system that covered the top of the head. It was a lightweight helmet and became quite popular. It is still being produced by Galibier and is useful for deflecting small blows.

When leading U.S. climbers opened their own distribution firms for European-manufactured climbing gear, climbing helmets were among the items imported. Some of the imported helmets were the JB, the Ultimate, the Interalp, and the Simond. Some German-made helmets were also imported and are still available here.

In California, Royal Robbins had a helmet custom made

to meet the special needs of climbers in Yosemite Valley. It consisted of a blue cap with a plastic shell molded into the top section of the cap. It was excellent for protection and a good sun visor. However, these were available for only a few years and are collectors' items now.

Choosing and Using a Climbing Helmet

Safety and protection are the most important things to look for when selecting your climbing helmet. The very best helmets, and those which offer the greatest amount of head protection, are those with a strong shell and a good inner suspension system. The inner suspension rests against the head. It keeps the outer shell away from the head and, thus, offers a much greater safety margin than a helmet which is merely a shell without an inner suspension.

Adjustability is another important thing to look for when selecting a helmet. This is particularly true if you want to use the same helmet in the summer and winter because you don't want to buy a separate helmet for every season. In the winter you will be wearing a Balaclava or other type of thick woolen hat underneath the helmet; so the winter helmet must be larger to fit over the warm hat. Another factor to consider when choosing a helmet for winter climbing is warmth. A lightweight shell without an inside lining will not be as warm as a shell with a lining. However, if you want your helmet for rock climbing in warmer seasons only, an unlined helmet may suit you perfectly.

All climbing helmets are made from a molded synthetic material; there are no metal climbing helmets. This is a point which should have been made to one of our students a few years ago. Before beginning a climb, we had discussed the possibility of being struck by lightning while climbing. I had told the students that just before lightning strikes, one can feel a slight tingling in his body. If a climber recognizes this tingling feeling, he should immediately remove all metal objects he might be wearing. Later, during the climb, I saw a helmet from one of my students careening to the ground. I was told afterward that the student had thought he felt the described tingling and, thinking his helmet was metal, had immediately dispatched it off the wall. End of helmet, but, fortunately, not of student, whose tingling was most likely only a good case of the jitters.

Market Update

There are several good climbing helmets now being manufactured and distributed in the United States. Probably the best is that made by Mountain Safety Research. The MSR helmet, which has been widely used for six years, is made from a material called Lexan, which does not crack upon impact. Its inner suspension system distributes the shock from a blow over the entire head. The MSR helmet has excellent side-to-side rigidity, making it extremely strong. It has a rim lined with foam, which helps absorb an impact and cushion the head. There are no protruding knobs or buttons on its outside. It has ventilation holes. The MSR is available in orange, blue, and yellow, and can usually be found at mountaineering stores. A special note: Lexan does not tolerate blended paints. The manufacturer warns against painting the helmet or using adhesives or solvents, which may contain acetone or toluene. These could weaken the shell's structure.

Mountain Safety Research will replace without charge any helmet that has been damaged in an accident. Of course, the manufacturer would like to receive an account of the accident, and the helmet must be returned before a replacement will be issued. The only disadvantage to

MSR helmet. (Courtesy of Mountain Safety Research, Inc.)

owning an MSR helmet is that they are not adjustable, therefore not suitable for both rock and ice climbing with the same helmet.

The Premier Climbing Helmet, sold by Recreational Equipment, Inc., in Seattle, is also made from molded Lexan. It has a nylon harness with an adjustable chin strap that permits easy removal of the helmet without complete unfastening. A nice feature of the Premier is that it has removable, adhesive foam strips which allow adjustability for sizes 6⅜ through 7¾. By removing the foam strips, one can use it over a woolen hat in the winter. The Premier is a good choice; it provides good safety protection at a reasonable price. It is a wise purchase for budget-minded climbers.

Another helmet that is somewhat inexpensive, yet of high quality and good design, is the Simond climbing helmet. This is the lightest available helmet that provides substantial head protection. Unfortunately, it is not available in American stores; one must order it directly from the manufacturer in France.

The Ultimate Helmet, distributed in the United States by Royal Robbins, was designed to be light yet comfortable. The Ultimate offers good protection, and is one of the strongest helmets available in this country. The shell is made from handlaid, reinforced fiberglass. It has an inner, nonabsorbent padding. Manufactured in England, it meets the British Standard Institute specifications. It weighs only 1 pound, 5 ounces. The Ultimate is available in two adjustable sizes: standard, which fits sizes 6⅝ through 7¼; and large, which fits sizes 7⅛ and larger. This helmet is a good choice for serious climbers and is highly recommended.

My favorite helmet is the Joe Brown, which we've been using for the past seven years with our students. It is manufactured by Snowdon Mouldings in England and is distributed by Climb High in Burlington, Vermont. It is entirely handmade; twenty separate steps comprise the manufacturing process. Mo Antoine, head of Snowdon and a leading Alpine climber, personally participates in the handcrafting process. He will also custom-design a helmet to your specifications.

The Joe Brown is available in two models. The lightweight model is made of fiberglass and has an internal suspension system. The heavyweight model is larger, lined with foam, also made of fiberglass, and also has an adjustable inner suspension system. The heavier model provides more ear protection, yet does not block out sound. In a recent test of eighteen climbing helmets used in Europe, conducted by the German Alpine Club, the Joe Brown was the only one to pass all of the shock absorbency tests. It is available in small, sizes 6½ to 6⅞; medium, sizes 6⅞ to 7¼; and large, sizes 7¼ to 7⅝. If a Joe Brown helmet should be damaged in an accident, Climb High will replace it free of charge upon receiving the damaged helmet and details of the accident.

Joe Brown helmet.
(Courtesy of
Paul Ross, International
Mountain Equipment.)

Another climbing helmet which we have had occasion to use is the Interalp. This is lightweight with no inner suspension system. Since it is a shell only, the shock of a blow can be transferred directly to the skull. It is available in small, medium, and large. It fits nicely and has an adjustable chin strap. The Interalp is a good helmet for beginning climbers to use at practice sessions.

6

Boots

A Little Background History

Items that played a key role in the evolution of mountaineering boots were nails, hemp rope, and rubber. The first step of the evolution from ordinary, leather-soled mountaineering shoes to today's technological wonders was taken when climbers started "nailing their boots," or adding small metal traction cleats to the soles. The cleats provided a better grip on rock and ice, and were actually the forerunners of today's Vibram-soled boots, which, when first developed, followed the grid pattern used with the early nails. Nailed boots were used widely in mountaineering. They were still in use as late as 1938 in America, as evidenced by an *Appalachia Journal* article by A. Gardner Dean that discusses the virtues of special European steel cleats called Tricounis.

Another step in the evolution occurred when climbers, realizing that heavy nailed boots were unsuitable for very delicate rock climbing, began climbing barefoot or in stocking feet, then added coils of hemp rope to the bottom of a normal, soft shoe. These rope-soled shoes became known generically as *scarpe da roccia,* Italian for "rock shoes."

Climbers then used a dual system; they climbed in nailed or cleated boots to the point where the rock became too difficult and steep, then switched to the scarpe da roccia. The hemp-rope coils allowed a good grip on rock and actually made possible many new technical ascents in Europe.

Early leading American climbers, including Miriam and Robert Underhill, William House, Paul Blanchard, and Ma and Pa Greenman, climbed in Red Ball sneakers, made of canvas and rubber. When Miriam Underhill visited Europe on a climbing excursion, she surprised her European climbing partners by being able to maneuver up routes in her Red Ball sneakers with their rubber soles that they could not begin to handle in their scarpe da roccia. The ability of the rubber to grip the rock on a steep friction climb was obviously far superior to that of the rope coils. Thus the standard Red Ball sneaker is the immediate predecessor of today's fancy rock-climbing shoe.

While Americans were scaling the heights in their Red Ball sneakers, French climbers began developing a shoe specifically for technical rock climbing. The first good shoe designed for this purpose was the PA shoe, manufactured by Galibier in France. News of its existence spread, and during the 1930s the PA became the most popular rock-climbing shoe in England as well as in France. The PA was designed with a rubber sole that was good for gripping the rock and also for edging.

During World War II the U.S. Army mountain troops wore heavy, sturdy boots with Vibram lug soles patterned after the early cleats.

Another early climbing shoe was the klettershuh. Manufactured in Germany and Austria, it was particularly popular with climbers in Yosemite. The klettershuh took early American climbers up the Nose of El Cap, the North American Wall, and many of the now classic routes.

Royal Robbins, one of the most prolific American climbers in the 1950s and 1960s, designed the first all-American rock-climbing shoe. Manufactured in France by the Galibier Company, the RR Yosemite combined the rigidity of an Alpine boot with the flexibility of the klettershuh. A rubber cap was added to the toe and heel to facilitate jamming.

The RR Yosemite was superbly designed for use on the vertical walls of Yosemite, and it became *the* climbing shoe of America throughout the '60s and early '70s. You were considered a real cragsman if you appeared at climbing areas wearing a pair of Royal Robbins shoes, something I was able to capitalize on as a beginning climber by being lucky enough to find a pair at a thrift shop for only one dollar. They had been left there by a climber who, because of a climbing accident, swore off the sport and turned in his gear. Proudly wearing my new purchase, I walked up to the base of a route on Cathedral Ledge. On my way, I passed two local cragsmen. Seeing the Robbins, one of them asked me, "What are you off to do today?" I answered naively, "I don't know, I'm just going to pick something and do it." A strange look, which I would not understand until a few years later, crossed his face. He hadn't the foggiest idea who I was; I could have been one of the Yosemite climbers visiting the area to steal some of his possible first ascents. Later, at the top of the cliff, after completing our climbs, I met him again. He looked at my boots and grudgingly asked, "Are they any good?" I smiled and said, "the best I've ever used." He said, "ever used?" I said, "Yeah, I just bought them at a thrift shop for a dollar." I then introduced myself as a beginning climber from the area. A wonderful smile of relief spread over his face, and we discussed the merits of the Robbins shoes. I learned later that I'd been talking to Joe Cote, author of the guidebook to Cathedral Ledge and one of the leading New Hampshire climbing pioneers.

As climbers began to push the standards higher and higher, approaching the 5.11 mark, the boot that became popular was the EB (or Ego Booster). Its soft and supple sole allowed adhesion to the rock with seemingly no effort. It seemed a climber wearing these boots did not need to worry any longer about the shape of the wall or small outcroppings for stances. He merely had to stick these fantastic miracle boots against anything to become an instant mountain goat. All good climbers changed to the EB and wore nothing else. These shoes made possible many of the routes being climbed today.

Choosing and Using Climbing Boots

There are basically four types of climbing shoes:

1. Mountaineering boots for high altitude expeditions or cold weather use, usually made of leather with an inner boot, and in some cases, two inner boots. The latest cold-weather boots on the market are made of plastic; we will discuss these later.
2. Heavy-duty mountaineering rock- and ice-climbing boots, made of leather with a Vibram sole designed for attachment of crampons.
3. A lightweight klettershuh, or shoe with flexible leather with a light Vibram sole, designed for rock climbing.
4. A sneakerlike shoe with a soft rubber sole.

For delicate rock climbing, the klettershuh and friction sole boot are appropriate. In higher mountains, the single-weight rock and mountaineering boot is used. For Alpine climbs, the double boot is necessary for warmth. For rock climbing only, a smooth sole boot is your best choice; for climbs with long approaches and long descents, boots with a Vibram sole, or at least a Vibram heel, will be more useful and comfortable.

It is important when fitting a rock-climbing shoe to make sure that it fits tightly, but not too tightly. It should be comfortable, not painful. Too often, a new climber is told by his friends to get his shoes "real tight," and is sorry later. When buying heavy mountaineering boots for winter climbing, wear two pairs of heavy woolen socks to get the proper fit. Make sure there is room to wiggle your toes. You can get a good case of frostbite if your boots fit too tightly and the circulation is cut off in your toes. There should be at least ½-inch of space between the toe of your foot and the toe of your boot. Your salesman will be able to help you if he is knowledgeable. Better yet, take an experienced climber with you for advice.

Care and Maintenance

Leather boots are easily affected by silicone waterproofing spray. Silicone softens the leather and should, therefore, be avoided. It can also cause the sole to delaminate. A product called Technical Waterproofing Compound, sold by Dartmouth Outdoor Sports, has no silicone in it and is excellent for waterproofing your boots.

Early Winters Limited in Seattle sells a product for sealing and waterproofing the welt of the boot—the part where the stitching contacts with the bottom laminates of leather. We have found that, on new shoes, several thin applications of Shoo Goo or Shoe Patch worked into the bottom of the leather seams with the end of a pencil make an excellent seal. Put this on the toe of your boots also; it will protect the leather from scuffs. Shoo Goo can also be used to repair rips and tears in friction climbing boots.

Store your boots in a cool, dry place. Moisture will

cause mildew and rot; heat will crack the leather. Spraying the inside of the shoe with a fungicide helps prevent internal rot.

Major Repairs

During our travels around the country we've had the opportunity to visit several cobblers and to get a look at their shops. Steve Komito is perhaps the best-known of all. His shop in Estes Park, Colorado, is the meeting place for all visiting and local climbers. Besides repairing boots, Steve has a wealth of information on local crags and the history of the area, as well as on care and maintenance of

Below and opposite, *Steve Komito's boot repair shop.*
(Courtesy of Steve Komito.)

boots. He has a long waiting list, so it's best to make arrangements in advance for him to repair your boots.

In Boulder, Colorado, Gary Neptune runs Neptune Mountaineering, a small climbing shop and boot repair service. Gary has done extensive climbing in the Boulder area and is full of information on local activities. His prices for repairs are competitive, and he does excellent work. Over the years, Chris Ellms, one of NCMI's instructors, has sent all of his boots to Gary. Once Gary rebuilt a pair of Royal Robbins rock-climbing shoes for Chris, using the new Vasque Ascender II soles. Chris says the shoes are much better with the addition of these soles, and he uses them for all of his aid-climbing classes.

Niall McGinnis, at Mountain Boot Repair in Ketchum, Idaho, has rebuilt several of my Galibier boots and has done an excellent job of reconditioning them. He can and does repair any and all types of boots and shoes.

In the East the best shoe repair service I am aware of is Leon Greenman's boot repair service at Down East on Spring Street in Manhattan. This is not just a boot repair service; Leon will service and custom construct tents, haul bags, and packs, will sew in zippers and fix all kinds of miscellaneous things that climbers always seem to require. Leon recently modified a pair of Chouinard Super-gators for me, and I was very pleased with the results.

All boot repairmen warn that it is very important to bring your boots for repair *before* the outer sole is worn completely through. Repairing a Vibram sole which has worn into the inner sole is difficult and expensive.

Should you want to contact any of these boot craftsmen by phone or mail, here is the information you'll need:

Steve Komito
Komito Boot Repair
Box 2106
Estes Park, Colorado 80517
(303) 586-5391

Gary Neptune
Neptune Mountaineering
1750 30th Street
Boulder, Colorado 80301
(303) 442-3551

Niall McGinnis
Mountain Boot Repair
P.O. Box 94
Ketchum, Idaho 83340
(208) 726-9935

Leon R. Greenman
Down East
93 Spring Street
New York, New York 10012
(212) 925-2633

Market Update

Asolo boots are relative newcomers to the American climbing market. In designing a boot to meet the specific needs of American climbers, Asolo enlisted the aid of Steve Komito. Asolo's two best boots are the Pro and the Cervino.

The top of the Asolo line is the Pro, a cold weather, double mountaineering boot. The inner boot is lined with synthetic fleece and reinforced with leather. It has a Norwegian welt, Celastic toe box, heel counter, and a PVC insole that gives the boot rigidity without any metal to transmit cold or increase weight. A Pro, size 8, weighs 3.70 kilograms. It is available in sizes 7 through 16, in medium and wide widths. The wide width fits an E-width foot comfortably. Reports on the Pro for cold weather mountaineering have been good.

The Cervino is a single-weight, technical mountaineering boot made from one piece of very heavy leather. Like the Pro, it is constructed on a Norwegian welt, with Celastic toe box and heel counter. It has a full steel shank for rigidity when using crampons. The weight of the boot in size 8 is 2.63 kilograms. It is available in sizes 7 to 16, in medium and wide widths. I've had no personal experience with the Cervino, but Steve Komito assures us that it will handle well in lightweight, technical mountaineering situations and when crampons are used.

Galibier boots are manufactured by Richard-Pontvert, S.A., a French mountaineering firm with a long history. For the past two decades, Galibier boots have been the leading boots for major high altitude expeditions and Alpine climbs. Galibier produces the widest and most comprehensive line of technical mountaineering boots available.

For the technical climber, Galibier introduced a brand new boot to their line this past year called the Contact. It is available in two heights: conventional, above the ankle; and with the height of a track shoe, below the ankle. The track shoe design is called the RP Contact. Since most technical rock climbers don't lace their shoes much past the ankle anyway, Galibier decided to experiment with a shorter shoe. Forty pairs of RP Contacts were brought into the United States for testing. Initial reports are that they are excellent. Their biggest advantage is that they are lightweight and easy to carry. I'm sure we will be seeing more and more of them.

Galibier makes two other fine shoes, the PA and the RR Varappe. The PA is a new version of the traditional PA, with a softer rubber sole and a wider last that is good for Americans with their wide feet. This is an excellent and economical rock-climbing shoe. It is available in half-sizes from 3 to 13.

The RR Varappe gives slightly more rigidity for edge climbing than the PA. The design is similar, but the last is much narrower. This shoe has replaced the RR Yosemite

Galibier Contact.
(Courtesy of Robbins Mountaingear.)

RR Varappe.
(Courtesy of Robbins Mountaingear.)

in the Galibier line of boots. One of its nice features is that it comes with elastic laces, which insure a continuously snug fit. The RR Varappe is available in sizes 2 to 13.

For high altitude mountaineering Galibier's Makalu is a leader and is probably the most widely used double boot in the world. It's been on countless expeditions to Nepal, South America, Alaska, and the high mountains of Canada. The Makalu is made with a heavy-duty leather construction laminated to composition board for rigidity. It uses a Norwegian welt with overlapping flat gusset to keep snow from entering the boot. The inner boot has a man-made fleece lining with leather top and a 2-inch scree cap, which also helps to prevent snow from entering. An optional liner of leather and felt is available separately. The Makalu has been proven to be the best leather double mountaineering boot available.

The Galibier Super Guide and Super Pro models are extremely popular and have seen many ascents. Both are good choices for winter mountaineering and are extremely good for rock climbing. I've used Galibier boots for many years and have been very pleased with them. The only drawback in them is that they are very narrow; if you have a wide foot you will not be able to wear Galibiers.

Kastinger ski boots have been well-known for many years. The A and T Company of Seattle is now importing Kastinger mountaineering boots. The Kastinger high altitude Messner Himalaya Ski Mountaineering Boot, which climbed to the top of Mt. Everest on the feet of Reinhold Messner and Peter Habeler, is revolutionizing high altitude mountaineering footwear. This is the most advanced and sophisticated boot we have ever had on our feet. Designed for ski mountaineering, it looks like a conventional downhill ski-boot. Its application to high altitude mountaineering is a major breakthrough.

The Himalaya's two-piece light plastic shell permits

Makalu.
(Courtesy of Robbins Mountaingear.)

easy forward flexibility for walking; yet, after clamping
down an adjustable buckle on the back · of the boot, it
becomes very stiff, giving substantial support for steep,
downhill ski-runs. The removable inner boot is wool lined
with foil in the toe, which reflects heat back to the toes, a
very good feature for added warmth. When Messner and
Habeler reached the summit of Everest in May, 1978,
wearing this boot, they experienced no frostbite at all.
Messner says, "Plastic boots will be the mountaineering
boot of the future for high altitude climbing." The Messner
Himalaya is available in sizes 6 through 13, in a medium
width. Total weight of the boot is 7 pounds, 8 ounces.
    Another revolutionary Kastinger boot is the Habeler

Above, *Galibier Super Pro.*
Below, *Galibier Super Guide.*
(*Courtesy of Robbins Mountaingear.*)

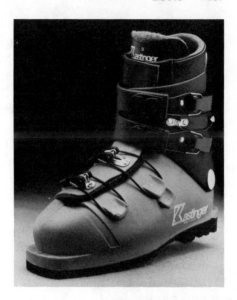

*Kastinger Messner Himalaya.
(Courtesy of A and T Ski Company.)*

*Kastinger Habeler Superlight.
(Courtesy of A and T Ski Company.)*

Special Superlight technical mountaineering boot, which I field-tested during the winter of 1978/79. Besides being the lightest single-weight boot I've ever used—5 pounds, 4 ounces—it is also one of the stiffest boots I've worn. I've broken down several pairs of boots over a season's use in the past; the Habeler didn't even show signs of wear after an entire season. The external skeleton of specially reinforced leather totally eliminates the possibility of leather collapse, and therefore it is impossible for crampon straps to crush in on the feet. The boot incorporates a specially laminated wooden insole, which gives it greater rigidity and saves on weight. It is constructed from four-grain millimeter leather with a very high wax content. It has an overlap gussetted tongue with a built-in Velcro fastener. The Habeler is available in sizes 6 through 13, medium width, which fits wide feet. This is one of the very best boots available.

A third Kastinger boot is the Expedition, a cold-weather, leather, technical mountaineering boot with a leather inner boot. The inner boot, like the Himalaya, has heat-reflecting foil laminated between layers of leather and wool felt. The external boot is of heavy, full-grain leather, flesh side out. The boot is triple-stitched and constructed on a Norwegian welt. It is available in sizes 7 through 13, men's medium width, and weighs 7 pounds, 8 ounces. Some climbers feel that, at this time, the Expedition may be the best leather double mountaineering boot available in America.

Most climbers consider the EB (nicknamed the Ego Booster) to be the best for pure technical rock climbing. This boot is completely flexible, has no shank, and is totally unpadded. It has an extremely narrow last. The rubber is very soft on the sides and bottom, which gives the EB an amazing adhesive quality on rock walls. Many of the new routes pioneered in recent years would have been impossible without EBs. It is definitely one of the very best rock-climbing shoes available.

*Kastinger Expedition
boot. (Courtesy of A and T
Ski Company.)*

I first became acquainted with Kleber boots during the summer of 1977 while guiding a party of clients on Cannon Cliff. A friend, who was wearing Klebers, said he felt they were the best he had worn for rock climbing and far superior to the EB in construction, design, and durability. I don't know that I share his superlative praise. The Kleber has the same flexibility and sticking qualities as the EB for severe friction climbs. And it edges wonderfully, but the toe is somewhat larger than the EB, making it a bit difficult to place in a very thin crack. It does have better adhesive qualities on wet rock than does the EB. The Kleber has a leather cup and sides and a reinforced back. It is available in sizes 5 through 12. One advantage over the EB is that it has a wider last, making it suitable for big-footed Americans. Whether it is as good as or better than the EB, the Kleber is an excellent rock-climbing shoe, and we highly endorse it.

The Vasque Ascender II combines the flexibility and smearing ability of the EB-type rock-climbing shoe with

EB, Kleber, and Summit boots.
(Courtesy of Climb High, Inc.)

the more conventional design of the klettershuh. A modified version of the conventional Vibram lug sole is one of
the keys to this boot's success. It is very similar to a
friction-sole boot, with a heel designed in a Commando
block style, which makes it good for wearing on approaches to climbs as well as on descents. The insole of
the Vasque Ascender II is molded for lateral support and
flexibility. This shoe is very comfortable and is good for
hard free climbing and aid climbing. It is all leather and is

Vasque Ascender II.
(Courtesy of Vasque.)

resoleable. It is available in sizes 7 through 10, in B, D, and EE widths. For a versatile, all-around climbing shoe, this is a very good choice.

The Fabiano Boot Company is currently making a double expedition boot of top grain leather with a fur-lined scree collar and a completely fur-lined, leather inner boot. This boot is very stiff, yet allows flexibility while walking. It's a large, heavy boot, most at home on ice and snow. Because of its size and weight and because it is not a rigid boot, it is not as good for vertical ice climbing. It is available in sizes 7 through 13. The Fabiano Double Expedition boot is a good choice if you are looking for durability and warmth.

Probably the most interesting mountaineering boot yet is that made by the Euro-Linea Company in Italy. There are so many wonderful features of this boot of the future

Fabiano Double Expedition Boot.
(Courtesy of Fabiano Shoe Company, Inc.)

that it will be hard to list them all. The outer boot is made from molded plastic in two parts, a base and a shank. It has a standard, lace fastening system; the manufacturer concluded that this was the best type of closure to tighten the boot at many points of the foot without creating pressure in any one place. The tongue, when tightened down with the lacing system, guarantees an absolutely waterproof boot. The sole of the boot follows the traditional mountain tread design and is vulcanized directly onto the base of the boot. There is no stitching; the vulcanization guarantees maximum strength. The sole of this boot should last much longer than that of a traditional mountaineering boot. It is also completely waterproof.

An internal shoe is made of soft leather, completely removable, and is covered with anti-tear nylon firmly anchored to the casing by Velcro strips on the ankle. This inner boot is fully padded with a micro-cellular material of varying thickness, according to the shape of the foot. At the rear of the inner boot there is a slot to hold a removable piece designed to give greater rigidity for descents. There is also a built-in gaiter, which not only makes the boot waterproof, but also seals it completely.

The Euro-Linea boot has many advantages over traditional leather boots. It is strong, yet lightweight. No waterproofing or sealing is necessary. Crampons cannot crush the permanently molded plastic. The plastic toe and heel do not scuff. The boot is rigid enough for ice-climbing of the highest standard, and also functions extremely well on rock faces. Unfortunately, the boot is not yet being sold in the United States; one must contact Euro-Linea in Italy directly. However, we are certain that the boot will soon be available here and that this boot, like the Kastinger, Messner, and Habeler, represents the mountain-climbing boot of the future.

Overboots

In some parts of the country, it is far too cold in the winter for only a lightweight, single mountaineering boot. In New Hampshire, for example, on Mount Washington, the weather may vary over a 50-degree range during the course of a day's climb. More than once, I left the Harvard Cabin early in the morning with temperatures in the low twenties, and by nightfall it was well below zero with fierce winds making it seem even colder. Warm feet and prevention of frostbite are major considerations in Alpine conditions. If you want more warmth and insulation than a single-weight boot can provide, but don't want the heaviness of a double boot, then overboots, or "super-gaiters," as they have become generically termed, are the answer.

Mike Brochu, an NCMI guide who has put in two seasons on McKinley, prevents frostbite by using a standard, Expedition double boot and two pairs of woolen socks layered with a pair of neoprene diving socks. The neoprene, in effect, turns the boot into a vapor barrier boot. Mike uses this with a supergaiter and says it is the best system for warmth in high-altitude climbing he has ever used. He cautions that to ensure a good fit socks should be worn when trying on a pair of these boots.

An excellent overboot is the Millet model 899. It is made with a heavy-duty, cotton canvas outer shell and a woolen lining. This overboot is stapled or nailed directly to the climbing boot. The overboot and boot, once nailed together, can be left as a permanent climbing combination, or they can be unnailed so that the overboot can be attached to other boots; the nail holes will not damage the boot. Attaching the gaiters with nails solves a problem common to other gaiters—namely, the tendency to slip off the toe of a boot, thereby allowing snow to pile up between overboot and shoe. With the Millet overboot, this is not a worry.

The Millet overboot has a front zipper opening which makes it very easy to reach inside to adjust or tighten the boots.

The bottom part of the Millet overboot is made of a tough, waterproof material which resists wear caused by lashed on crampons or rock abrasion.

A good waterproof combination of boot and overboot can be made by nailing the overboot to the shoe and then applying a generous amount of Shoo Goo all around the attachment.

Chouinard Supergators, originally designed and produced by Peter Carman of Jackson Hole, Wyoming, have gained wide popularity and use over the past years. There

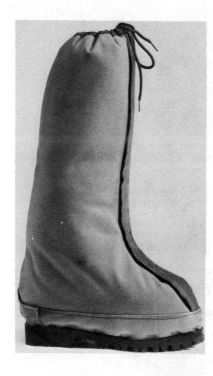

Millet Overboot.
(Courtesy of Sacs Millet S.A.)

are two Supergator models available—the original, and a new design. The original Supergators were put on before the boots were put on. They were then pulled down over the boots and lashed to the boots with a neoprene buckle that passed under the instep of the boot.

The bottom edge of the Supergator, which surrounds the welt of the boot, is protected by heavy-duty, nylon tape. The toe of the Supergator does slip off the boot, allowing snow to be trapped underneath. An attempt to correct this was made by the use of small eye hooks, but they broke and fell off.

The new Chouinard Supergator is very well designed and also very warm, made of nylon. It has a front-zipper opening, an addition I find most welcome. In fact, before the new model was made available, I had my older pair

Chouinard Supergators.
(Courtesy of Great Pacific Iron Works.)

modified by Leon Greenman of Down East, as I mentioned earlier. Leon put in a full front zipper from the knee to the toe and covered it with a waterproof placket insulated with foam and secured by Velcro strips.

Peter Carman now manufactures a supergaiter under his own label. The Carman supergaiter uses a mechanical tightening device to solve the problem of toe lifting. The device is hidden behind a Velcro closure on the sides of the gaiter. A metal cable totally surrounds the bottom of the boot; when tightened the cable is drawn snugly under the welt of the shoe and remains secure during use. This

Expedition overboot.
(Courtesy of Pak Foam Products.)

eliminates toe slippage problems and also permits the climber to use different sizes of boots. Outer shapes and sizes of boots vary considerably—a size 10 Kastinger boot is not the same size as a size 10 Galibier—so the adjustability feature of the Carman overboot is a definite plus.

The three overboots discussed above are designed for technical rock and ice climbing in that they leave the boot sole exposed. For climbing where a Vibram sole is not necessary, the best expedition overboot I know of is made by Pak Foam Products in Pawtucket, Rhode Island. It is a full overboot, which covers the top part as well as the sole of the boot. The top part of the boot is Gore-Tex, the bottom is completely insulated with a new 3M product called Thinsulate. The lower boot is made of heavy-duty Cordura nylon and has a removable Ensolite lining. Three pieces of 2-inch nylon webbing are sewn onto the welt of the boot to protect the toe and instep from abrasion. The

Forrest Expedition overboots. Polar Guard lined.
(Courtesy of Forrest Mountaineering.)

Expedition overboot slips on over the climbing boot and is closed with a front lacing system. There are no exposed seams, which minimizes heat loss. For climbs in Alaska or the Himalayas, or anywhere where there will be Alpine conditions, the Expedition overboot can save your feet from frostbite.

If you are unable to find the Pak Foam overboots, a good second choice is the Forrest Expedition Polar Guard overboot. The body of the shoe is insulated with Polar Guard. There are two removable Ensolite soles. The overboot has a front closing with laces and is made of reinforced Cordura nylon, which also fully encloses the climbing boot. It is fully insulated with a reflective material called Astrolar and removable Ensolite inner soles. This overboot has a front closing with laces. It is a good, sturdy, warm overboot.

7

Ice Tools

A Little Background History

The ice axe dates back as far as 1842, and perhaps further, to the Chamonix area of France where climbing guides used woodcutters' axes to aid their ascents of Mont Blanc. This long axe with a very large head was used to chop platform steps to make the climb up frozen snow and ice easier for tourists. At that time only the leading European guides carried an axe. The first Americans known to use an ice axe were probably the Heard brothers, who were photographed with their guide on Mont Blanc in 1857. By the 1920s, Chamonix guides were using shorter axes, but it took nearly a century for the ice axe to evolve from the traditional Alpenstock length, over 5 feet, to the size it is today.

After the axe was shortened in the '20s, the next major design change was not to take place until the early 1930s when European guides added teeth to the straight blade of the axe. The teeth allowed the axe to be more securely lodged in ice or hard snow.

In the early 1960s, Yvon Chouinard, while visiting Europe, realized that if the toothy blade were dropped at an angle it would provide more purchase; security on very steep terrain would be possible.

In the late 1960s, Colorado Mountain Industries introduced an axe with an aluminum shaft that was stronger and lighter than traditional wooden handles. However, climbers, who seem to be just as resistant to change as the rest of the population, didn't like the metal handles and wouldn't use them. It wasn't until Larry Penberthy of Mountain Safety Research conducted comparison tests and showed that wooden handles were definitely not as strong as aluminum-shafted ones that climbers realized the safety potential of aluminum. Today, almost all manufacturers produce aluminum-shafted ice axes, although wooden ones are still being made for those who enjoy the aesthetic appeal of natural woodgrain and the feel of wood. With the recent introduction of graphite and fiberglass handles, the full potential of which is just beginning to be known, wooden handles are becoming even more antique. I believe that within a few years wood-handled axes will be seen only in museums and on the walls of mountain chalets.

Choosing and Using Ice Tools

There are many different types of ice axes and hammers for different kinds of winter terrain. There are tools that allow climbers to ascend vertical ice pitches, or ice walls, hundreds of feet high, varying in steepness from 85 to 95 degrees. There are tools much better suited for general mountaineering terrain where pitches are no steeper than 60 degrees. There are tools that bridge the gap between the two. Ice tools come in a variety of shapes and sizes.

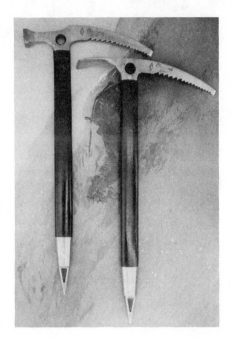

*Chouinard ice tools.
(Courtesy of Great
Pacific Iron Works.)*

Some have very steep drooped picks, such as the Terror-dactyl and the Simond Chacal; others, like the Sabre and Curver, have a less pronounced droop.

You should select an axe suitable for the type of climbing you will be doing. For general mountaineering, all you will need is an ice axe suitable for self-arrest. It should be long enough to be used as a balance tool when walking on glacial snows, and good for cutting an occasional step.

For vertical ice, a tool with a much shorter handle is essential. The standard length of a general purpose mountaineering axe is 70 centimeters. For vertical ice, 50-centimeter tools are much better. Before making your purchase, experiment with other climbers' axes to see which axe suits you best.

For steep vertical ice, it is necessary to carry at least two ice tools. Many climbers carry three because the

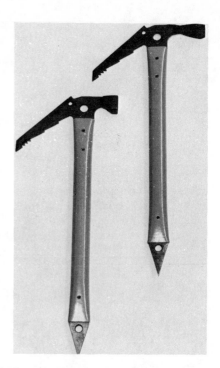

Forrest short ice tools. (Courtesy of Forrest Mountaineering.)

possibility of a tool breaking is very real; the third is used as a backup. One of these tools must have a hammer head for placing ice pitons or screws.

I learned about carrying a backup tool while soloing Mount Willard in Crawford Notch, New Hampshire. I was using two brand new tools, a North Wall hammer and an ice hammer. On the second pitch, the North Wall hammer broke at the connection of head and shaft. I continued the climb using only the ice hammer. When I took the hammer out of the ice on the fourth pitch, most of the blade stayed behind in the ice; I was left holding only the shaft. Two broken ice tools on one climb! There was nothing left for me to do other than finish the pitch with crampons only and traverse off the climb. Now I *always* carry three tools!

For climbing Mount Rainier, an 80- or 90-centimeter axe is all one needs. For climbing the Black Dike on Cannon

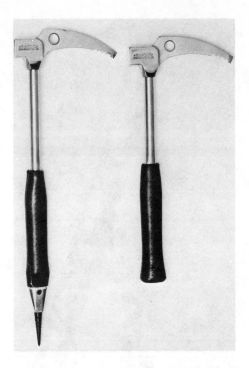

Simond tools with hammer heads. (Courtesy of ETS Claudius Simond et fils.)

Cliff, New Hampshire, two tools 50-centimeters long, one an Alpa-Mayo, the other a Forrest Mjollnir Hammer, would be recommended. Another very good combination of tools for the Black Dike is the Chouinard 60-centimeter Piolet and the Chouinard Ice Hammer. For an ascent of Recompense on Cathedral Ledge in New Hampshire, a Hummingbird and Terrordactyl are a good team. The steeper the terrain, the more variation the climber may need.

Buying a used axe is a good idea. The metal-shafted axe will last indefinitely. In this day of high technology, with new and innovative tools continuously being introduced, climbers frequently turn over, or "trade up," their equipment. With some items it isn't wise to buy second hand, but with ice axes it is perfectly safe and to your economic advantage to do so.

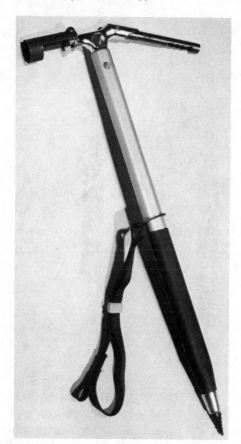

Hummingbird ice axe.
(Courtesy of
Lowe Alpine Systems.)

Right, *Clog ice tools.*
(Courtesy of Climb High, Inc.)

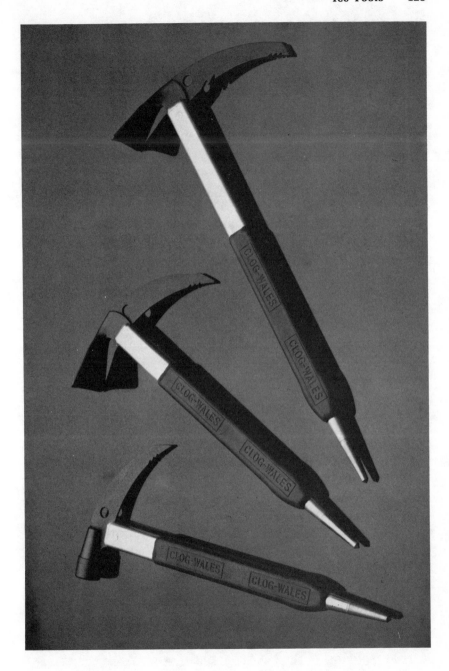

Care and Maintenance

Keep the blade and teeth of your ice axe razor sharp.
You can use a standard, bastard single-cut file to sharpen
the teeth yourself.

A light coating of oil or WD-40 silicone spray will help
prevent surface rust, and should be applied after your axe
has been cleaned and dried following a climb. To prevent
damage to your rucksack, or to you, keep your ice axe in a
protective sheath while in transit and during storage.
Spike and adze protectors are available from most mountaineering stores.

If your metal-handled ice axe does not have a rubber-
ized grip, strips of bicycle inner tubing wrapped around
and glued to the handle will provide a good grip and good
insulation. Blue cross-country ski wax rubbed on the shaft
will provide a better grip when wearing woolen gloves.

If your axe begins to show fatigue, to bend or deform, it
is time to buy a new one. If your axe should break in
normal use, return it to the store or manufacturer for a
replacement.

Market Update

Technology of today has come so far that there are
almost no bad ice tools being sold in America. Tools are
becoming ever more sophisticated, and the distinction
between tools is not so much one of quality as of design.
Each manufacturer is trying to produce a unique tool. A
big consideration is aesthetics. Climbers not only like to
use their tools, they *love* to admire and fondle them. So a
particularly nice-looking tool, which functions very well,
is the goal of manufacturers.

All of the Mountain Safety Research ice axes are made
from aircraft alloy aluminum tubing and have an innovative positive clearance angle to their picks (blades) com-

bined with a large hooking angle that requires less force when driving into snow and ice. MSR produces four very popular axes. The Thunderbird is a general purpose, glacial climbing axe. It weighs 1 pound, 15 ounces and is available in lengths that vary in one-inch increments from 26 to 37 inches. The Aluminum Head Thunderbird is very similar in design to the Thunderbird but weighs half a pound less. The Eagle, with a hooking degree of 68, is a good choice for general purpose mountaineering. The Eagle weighs 1 pound, 15 ounces. The Sumner, with a hooking angle of 53 degrees, weighs 1 pound, 11 ounces. You can always spot an MSR axe on snow or ice because they are blue. They are very good for modest ice climbing and leisure climbing, and are relatively inexpensive.

Simond produces one of the most complete lines of climbing axes of any manufacturer. The most interesting, the Condor and the Ice Hammer, both of which have hammer heads for knocking in ice screws, are almost identical. However, the Condor is longer and has a steel spike to be used for balance when surmounting bulges. The Condor is an excellent, intermediate-length ice-climbing hammer. It has seen a number of very difficult ascents, including the first ascent of the Diagonal on Cathedral Ledge—a very hard, grade-IV, mixed ice and snow climb. The Simond Ice Hammer is probably the best ice-climbing hammer that we can recommend for general purpose climbing, as well as for placement and removal of pitons.

Simond's newest ice tool, the Chacal, looks like a conventional climbing hammer. But it has several interchangeable picks. Besides a standard pick, which makes it an excellent North Wall hammer, it has two steep-drooped picks of different lengths and sizes. The smaller pick is almost identical to the Terrordactyl ice axe; the longer pick functions similarly to the Terrordactyl—with a downward-thrust placement—but is designed for Névé ice,

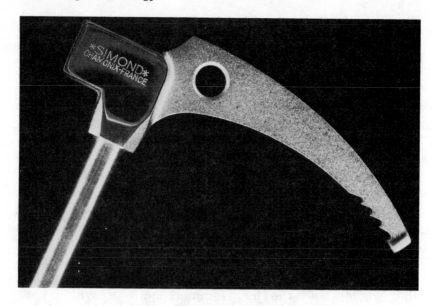

Above, Simond Ice Hammer.
(Courtesy of ETS Claudius Simond et fils.)

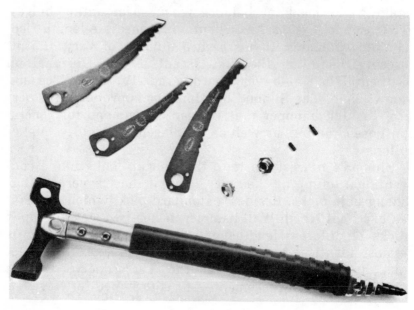

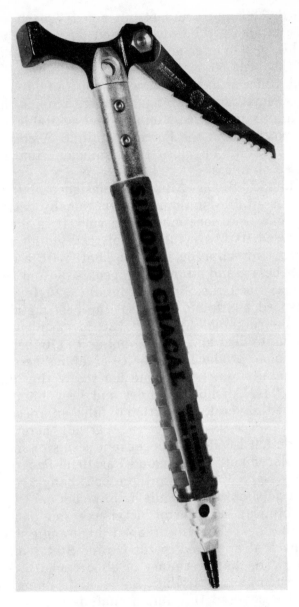

Left and above, *Simond Chacal*.
(Courtesy of ETS Claudius Simond et fils.)

which is much more compact but not as frozen as water ice. There is also a tube pick. I used the prototype of the Chacal this past winter on New England walls and found it to be the best 55-centimeter mixed climbing tool I've ever used. Since it has a hammer head, it is not necessary to carry a small ice-climbing hammer. This is probably the best multipurpose ice-climbing tool available, with the possible exception of the Forrest Mjollnir. A combination of the two would be more than sufficient for the most experienced climbers.

The Simond Super Mustang, designed by William Cecchinel, is an all-aluminum, conventionally designed ice axe for general purpose mountaineering. It is the lightest I've ever used. It has a full row of teeth going up to the shaft, a hole for clipping into the shaft with a carabiner for ice-axe belay, and an interchangeable bottom spike.

NCMI has used the Simond Metallic 720 for the past five years and has found it one of the best metal-shafted axes for instructional use. The 720 is excellent for the general mountaineer and the beginning ice climber.

Simond also produces three ice-climbing screws. The best is a tubular, nickel-chrome ice screw that displaces the ice. It has a hollow channel and very high threads. We've staged several instructional falls on these screws with great success. A drive-in Warthog screw is not desirable on hard water-ice because it seems to shatter the ice upon placement. The Simond Parallelle Progressive is an alternative to the now antique coat-hanger ice screw but is still no substitute for the hollow-channel ice screw.

The MacInnes Peck Terrordactyl axe and hammer are perhaps the best known drooped high-angle climbing-tools. They first appeared in the United States in the late 1960s and were the forerunner of all drooped-pick climbing tools, such as the Mjollnir, Sabre, and Simond Chacal. Their rubber-covered Duralumin shaft is triple-riveted to the 55-degree, angular pick. The pick is made of ⅛-inch,

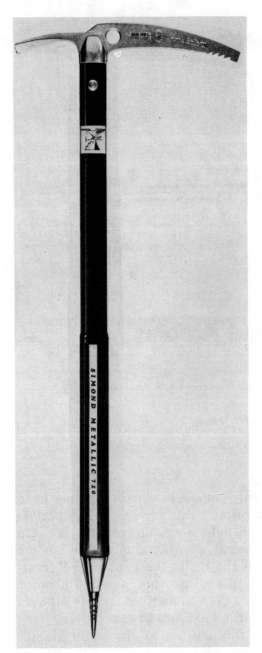

*Simond Super Metallic 720.
(Courtesy of ETS Claudius
Simond et fils.)*

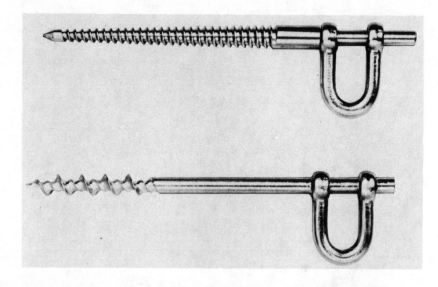

Simond Ice Climbing Screws.
(Courtesy of ETS Claudius Simond et fils.)

high-tensile stainless steel. The Terrordactyl hammer head is excellent for placing pitons; the adze model is perfect for cutting small, pigeon-hole steps in vertical ice. On steep mixed ice climbs, very often the climber finds snow plastered and frozen into the wall. The Peck adze Terrordactyl is excellent for cutting into this snow to provide anchorage. Peck tools have seen numerous ascents all over the world and are still in the forefront of tool design.

The Curver ice axe, manufactured by Snowdon Mould-

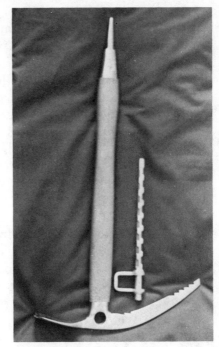

Curver ice axe and Super Hog
Ice Peg. (Courtesy of Paul Ross,
International Mountain
Equipment.)

ings in Wales, is an excellent tool for climbs similar to the
gully climbs of Scotland and Wales. The handle is made
from laminated, reinforced fiberglass with a sand finish,
which produces an excellent grip. At the end of the shaft
is a large bump to facilitate holding onto the tool on steep
ice. This tool may not be too well suited for American
climbing, but it is an excellent ice axe. It is available in
lengths progressing in 3-inch increments from 16 to 24
inches. Its total weight in the 16-inch size is 25 ounces.

Snowdon makes a drive-in, warthog-type ice screw
called the Super Hog Ice Peg. It is 8-inches long and
weighs 7 ounces. We've used this over the past five years
and find it the best drive-in, warthog-type tool still available in America.

Since the innovative Yvon Chouinard increased the
droop of the standard climbing axe, most manufacturers

have followed suit, and a very sharply curved ice axe is now the norm. Interalp manufactures for Chouinard's Great Pacific Iron Works two ice-climbing tools well worth noting, the Zero North Wall Hammer and the Zero Ice Axe. Both tools in short lengths are excellent for all types of ice climbing as well as for general mountaineering. The original Zero Ice Axe shaft was made of laminated bamboo, but in 1978 Chouinard switched to a reinforced man-made material.

Besides being an innovator in ice-axe design and modification, Chouinard came out with what is probably the best tubular ice screw available in the world, called Chouinard Tubular Screws. They are available in four sizes: 13, 17, 22, and 28 centimeters. The weight of a 22-centimeter screw is 5 ounces. They are excellently designed and one of the most secure anchors on vertical ice.

The Warthog is Chouinard's contribution to the redesign of conventional ice-climbing pitons. The Warthog, which is the best we have ever used, is no longer being manufactured because it was far too expensive to produce.

Forrest Mountaineering has the most diversified line of ice-climbing tools made in America. Like the Simond Chacal, the Forrest Mjollnir is a multiheaded ice hammer. I've used this hammer for five years now and have found that it is one of the most useful hammers I have tried. I now use it in conjunction with the Simond Chacal. It's good to be able to change heads on a long, mixed, Alpine ascent. The Mjollnir has four different picks: a tube pick, a skye pick, an ice pick, and a rock pick. Forrest axes are stamped from a single piece of metal with a twisted adze. Is this superior to a forged adze? This is a matter of debate. Quite simply, the Forrest axes are extremely strong, and their design is excellent.

Forrest axes have an aluminum shaft coated with a nonconductive vinyl material which helps to prevent cold hands. They are available in several models. The Névé is

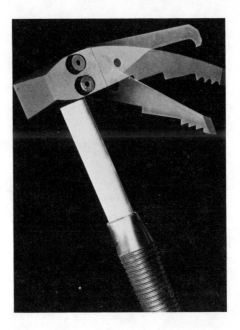

Forrest Mjollnir multihead ice hammer. (Courtesy of Forrest Mountaineering.)

a general purpose mountaineering ice axe designed for glacial walking. It is available in lengths that progress in 5-centimeter increments from 40 to 95 centimeters. The weight of an 80-centimeter Névé is 38 ounces.

The Forrest Verglas is designed for all-around mountaineering, from glacial climbing to vertical frozen waterfalls. It has a very good chisel point that provides penetration into hard water ice. It comes in 40- to 95-centimeter lengths. The 70-centimeter size weighs 36 ounces. If one wants to purchase a single axe for all types of climbing, the Verglas is probably the best made in America.

One of the nicer tools Forrest introduced this past winter is the Forrest North Wall Hammer, designed to be a companion to the Verglas. It easily sets ice screws and rock pitons into the wall with its head. The North Wall Hammer is designed for very steep ice climbing. For steep

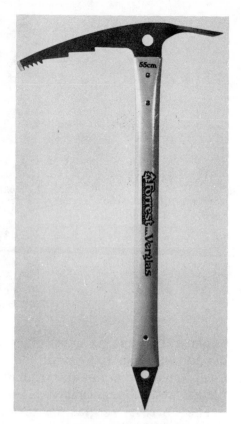

Forrest Verglas.
(Courtesy of
Forrest Mountaineering.)

waterfall ice the shortest variety should be used. It is available in 40- to 95-centimeter lengths; the lengths from 40 to 55 centimeters are best for steep ice climbing.

Forrest's steep-drooped axe is the Serac Sabre Axe. There is also a Serac Sabre hammer. The droop of the pick is similar to the Terrordactyl. Both axe and hammer work extremely well in steep terrain. We recommend that the lengths from 40 to 60 centimeters be used for steep terrain.

SMC makes a high-quality ice axe from drop-forge chrome-moly alloy steel. The head is heat treated and tempered to withstand severe abuse; the shaft is produced

from tubular aluminum alloy and has a PVC covering
which provides insulation. The curvature of the pick has
been designed for technical climbing on steep ice. We used
it and found it extremely heavy. However, it might be a
good investment for colleges and outing groups that want
to make their equipment last twenty or thirty years. It is a
very sturdy implement.

The ice axe most commonly found in mountaineering
stores is the Interalp, a familiar name for many years.
There are currently three Interalp models available. The

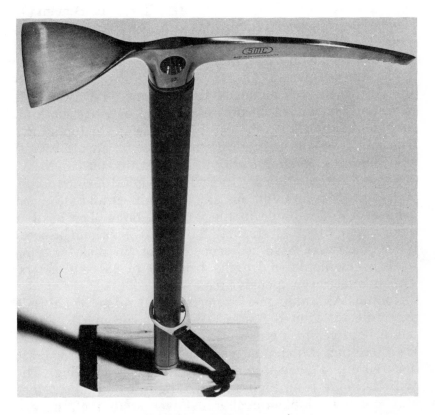

SMC ice axe. (Courtesy of
Seattle Manufacturing Corporation.)

most popular is the Cerro Torre, made from nickel chrome-moly steel, with a slightly curved adze. The pick has teeth and an aluminum shaft covered with plastic sheathing. It comes in 60- to 90-centimeter lengths.

The Interalp Alpa Mayo is probably a better choice than the Cerro Torre. The two axes are similar, but the Alpa Mayo features a flat adze, much better for chipping pigeon-hole steps. Also, the Alpa Mayo pick has a steeper bend. We've used the Alpa Mayo on ascents of the Black Dike, one of the harder ice climbs in the eastern United States. It is now available with a full set of teeth along the pick to the shaft, which facilitates placement in steeper terrain and candlestick ice. The Alpa Mayo is available in lengths from 55 to 90 centimeters. This is a good axe for technical climbing.

The third Interalp tool is the Fitz-Roy, an all-metal-shafted North Wall hammer—the first one I'd ever used. It is made from nickel chrome-moly steel and has teeth all the way to the shaft. The carabiner hole on the top allows belaying from the ice tool. It has a plastic sheath on the shaft, and it is available only in a 60-centimeter length.

A new introduction by Interalp, though difficult to find, is the Interalp Titanium ice axe, the lightest and strongest ice axe now available in the United States. The head is made from titanium steel. It has a flat adze and a carabiner hole; there is an accessory hole on the pick for tying in. It is available in lengths from 60 to 85 centimeters. This is a terribly expensive ice axe.

Robbins Mountaingear imports a full range of LaPrade axes into the United States. The LaPrade Super Huandoy has a lightweight metal shaft and is designed for vertical ice climbing. Maximum penetration and anchorage are ensured by a curved blade with double notching. The shaft is made from high-strength, light, metal alloy. Non-slip, corrugated plastic on the lower section of the axe insulates the hands from cold metal. The axe comes in lengths from 50 to 80 centimeters.

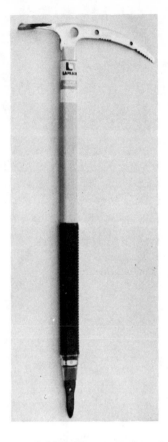

LaPrade Super Huandoy.
(Courtesy of Robbins Mountaingear.)

The Standard Huandoy is a lightweight version of the Super and is less expensive. It provides good penetration on less steep, less technical ice climbs. It is available in 50- to 80-centimeter lengths.

The LaPrade Randalp is another inexpensive ice axe. It is designed for step cutting, trekking, and snowclimbing. This is not an ice-climbing tool; it is specifically designed for mountain hiking and glacial travel.

Another axe distributed by Robbins is the Alpelit, made from zicral. The handle is covered with adiprene, which remains supple and soft to minus 50 degrees Fahrenheit. It is available in two models, the Standard, which has one

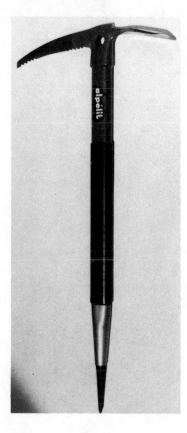

Alpelit ice axe.
(Robbins Mountaingear.)

set of teeth, and the Special, which has an extra set of teeth on the base of the pick. The Alpelit is very light, easy to use, and functional. It has a flat adze and is very good for all types of climbing. It comes in lengths from 60 to 90 centimeters. The 70-centimeter model weighs 1 pound, 11 ounces.

In the early 1970s, the Terrordactyl ice hammer was accepted by most American climbers as *the* vertical ice tool. One of its biggest drawbacks was that climbers invariably smashed their knuckles against the ice when setting the hammer in the ice; this happened because the blade was inserted fully to the hilt. A group of Colorado

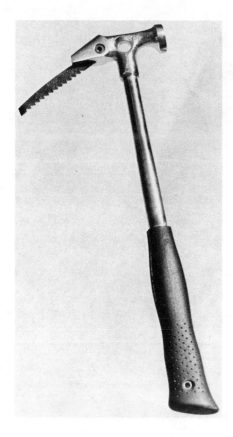

*Lowe Hummingbird hammer.
(Courtesy of
Lowe Alpine Systems.)*

climbers took the Terrordactyl design and made a new hammer called the Roosterhead, which solved the smashed knuckles problem. The Roosterhead has a bulbous spike low on the shaft, below where the hammer is held. The spike extends out farther than the hand and prevents the hand and knuckles from connecting with the ice. While preserving climbers' knuckles, however, the Roosterhead does have a few disadvantages. The protruding lower spike prevents it from being hung in a holster, and the spike also presents the possibility of jabbing the climber in the leg during a fall.

The Lowe brothers of Lowe Alpine Systems were the

Snarg ice piton.
(Courtesy of
Lowe Alpine Systems.)

first to recognize the advantages of a tubular pick for vertical ice climbing. All other models of ice axes displace and shatter ice as they penetrate a wall. The tubular pick allows ice to be displaced without cracking or shattering. A tubular pick goes in very softly, with a little popping sound, compared to the crashing and chipping and splintering of a conventional ice tool.

The Lowe Hummingbird axe and Hummingbird hammer both have interchangeable tube picks and Alpine picks. The axe, with a removable adze, becomes a North Wall hammer. The tubular pick allows secure placement on extremely brittle water-ice where other tools would glance off. The Lowe tools surely must go down on record as the most innovative climbing tools developed since the guides at Chamonix took their woodcutter axes up Mont Blanc.

This past year, Lowe Alpine Systems introduced a completely refined Snarg ice-climbing piton. It is a drive-in device, easily placed while hanging from one tool on steep vertical ice walls. The leader forms a small hole and drives the Snarg in up to the hilt. The second removes it by inserting his ice hammer and turning. The Snarg's unique cleaning slot allows repeated placement and eliminates freezing up problems common to all other tubular screws.

For protection and belays on Névé snow, climbers used to thrust an ice axe into the snow to provide an anchor. Lowe realized that a hollow tube would work better—the hollow tube displacing the snow, freezing in place, and

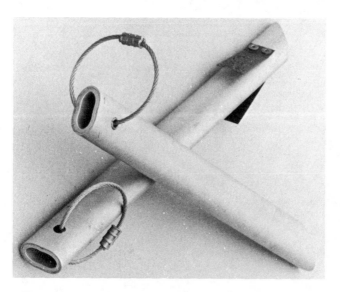

The Neve Picket.
(Courtesy of Lowe Alpine Systems.)

thus providing secure anchorage. The Lowe brothers designed and are now producing what they call a Neve Picket, which is essentially a hollow axe-shaft with side wings that help prevent the pick from dislodging from soft snow. It is a very handy item.

Rock climbing is a sport that can be learned quite easily by trial and error. Ice climbing is a far more arduous and dangerous undertaking. Conditions change daily. Ice may be affected by the cold, by warming, by mineral deposits, and by many other factors. To become an expert ice climber takes much practice. However, to start you on your way, there are two excellent books that provide a good foundation of knowledge about the vagaries of ice. The best of the two is by Jeff Lowe, one of the Lowe brothers, entitled *The Ice Experience*. The other is *Climbing Ice* by Yvon Chouinard. Both books will whet your appetite for firsthand experience on ice and snow, which we know will be thrilling and hope will be safe.

8

Crampons

A Little Background History

Unlike other mountaineering gear, crampons have been around in one form or another for a long time. In a December, 1940, *Appalachia Magazine* article on artificial aids in early mountaineering, J. Monroe Thorington wrote that crampons of various types and shapes were used in Europe from early days on. Early natives of the Caucasus wore sandles of untanned leather, soled with metal plates armed with spikes for crossing ice and snow. Iron foot spikes were used by Celtic miners from 700 B.C. to 400 B.C. Crampons used by the Gauls in Roman days can be seen at the Museum of Saint Germain-en-Laye.

In the late 1800s in Europe, lash-on crampons were worn over nailed climbing boots.

Prior to World War II, German and Austrian climbers developed a crampon with front points in addition to the bottom spikes. These were used on the North Wall of the

Eiger. After that successful climb, many manufacturers began to experiment with new designs and metals.

The flexible crampon was used in those days. A hinge in the middle of the crampon allowed it to bend with the climbing shoe. At that time boots were not rigid; so a flexible crampon was necessary.

When boots became more rigid to allow climbers to stand comfortably on steep ice terrain, a rigid crampon was developed to mate with the rigid boot. In the United States, Yvon Chouinard worked with the Salewa Company to produce the first commercial, rigid, mountaineering crampon. It opened America up for vertical ice exploration.

Choosing and Using Crampons

When purchasing crampons, your first consideration will be the type of boot the crampon will be mated with. A flexible boot needs a flexible crampon. The crampon needs to bend with the boot. Flexible crampons have either ten or twelve points. The twelve-point variety includes two front points, which should extend from ¾ to 1 inch out from the boots. The front points will be either straight or angled downward. The angled points are good for snow climbing and glacial work; straight points are for technical ice climbing.

For stiff boots, a rigid crampon is necessary. If your favorite pair of boots—very rigid when new—becomes softer and more flexible with years of wear, it will not work too well with a pair of rigid crampons. To solve this problem, Chris Rowins, one of NCMI's guides, traced the outline of the sole of his boot onto a piece of ¼-inch plywood, cut it out with a jigsaw, and now uses that piece of plywood in conjunction with a rigid crampon. The plywood does not permit the boot to flex, so his rigid crampon does not flex or break. And Chris can continue to wear his favorite, custom-made boots.

Along with choosing the proper crampons you must select good crampon straps. They should have strong and secure buckles to insure that the crampons won't fall off during a climb. The best strap material is reinforced neoprene nylon, which doesn't crack, stretch, freeze, or fall off during extreme technical climbs.

It takes awhile to get the hang of using crampons safely and effectively. The best advice I can offer is that, after reading several good instruction books, any climber interested in snow and ice climbing should receive instructions from a competent climbing school or guide.

Care and Maintenance

The care and maintenance of your crampons is important. After each climb, they should be carefully dried to prevent surface rust from building up. The spikes and points should be kept sharp with a good metal file. At the end of each climbing season, dismantle your crampons completely and spray all parts with oil or WD-40 to prevent corrosion. Make sure that the point protectors your crampons are placed in are completely free of moisture. If the crampons show signs of wear, or if you can spot fatigue cracks on them, you can either buy replacement parts for the damaged section or replace the entire crampon.

Market Update

Robbins Mountaingear imports two types of LaPrade/ Desmaison crampons, the Regular and the Super. Both are twelve-point crampons with two adjustments for proper and secure fit. They are made of cold rolled steel, which is light and extremely strong. The two adjustment systems allow the crampon to be used with either a flexible or rigid boot, a definite economic advantage, since one pair of crampons takes the place of two. Both models are avail-

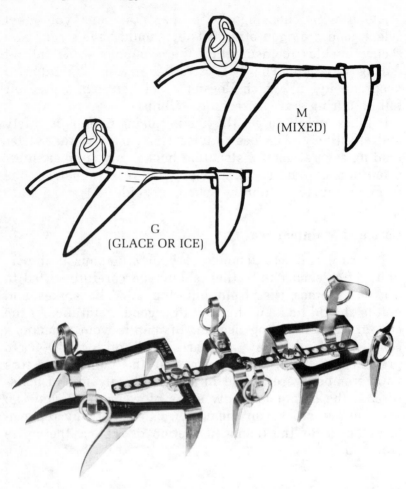

M
(MIXED)

G
(GLACE OR ICE)

LaPrade/Desmaison crampons.
(Courtesy of Robbins Mountaingear.)

able in two different shapes. One is particularly suitable
for mixed rock and ice climbing, the other for glacial and
ice climbing only. It is recommended that the glacial
crampon not be used for mixed climbing. The Regular
model is guaranteed against brittleness breakdown to 30
degrees below zero. The Super model is guaranteed to 60

below. Both models are individually numbered and uncon-
ditionally guaranteed by the manufacturer for two years
from date of purchase. Since they are adjustable, one size
fits boot sizes from 4 through 13. The weight of the
Regular model is 1 pound, 13 ounces; the Super weighs
two pounds.

The Chouinard crampon, manufactured by Salewa to
Chouinard's specifications, is a fully adjustable, rigid,
twelve-point crampon designed for vertical, technical ice
climbing. It is an extremely rigid crampon. The points are
very sharp and handle particularly well on mixed rock
and ice climbs. The Chouinard weighs 1 pound, 6 ounces
and will fit boot sizes 7 through 13. Smaller sizes are
available by special order.

The Salewa adjustable twelve-point crampon is probably the most popular of all adjustable crampons in the
United States. It has seen numerous climbs of the highest
standard. It can be used in temperatures to minus 40
degrees. Salewa crampons are available in sizes 5 to 14,
extra wide. They weigh, on the average, 600 grams.
Salewa is now making a crampon with reinforced
tungsten steel tips, called the Red Point Expedition. This
is only available in sizes 7½ through 12, in narrow,
medium, and wide widths.

Seattle Manufacturing Corporation's vertical crampon is
similar in design to the Chouinard but made of slightly
heavier metal. The problems of breakage are almost totally eliminated with the SMC crampon. It is guaranteed
by the manufacturer against defects and will be replaced
free of charge if defective. The lashing device of the rigid
SMC crampon is somewhat harder to use than that of the
Chouinard. An optional flip ring must be attached to the
front to facilitate attachment to very large double boots.
We've used them for several seasons of ice climbing; they
work and handle extremely well. SMC offers the rigid
crampon in both a blue and a bright finish, the blue being
a bit less expensive than the bright.

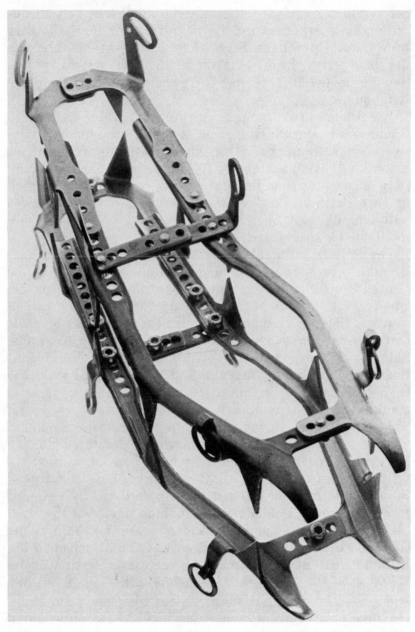

Chouinard/Salewa crampons.
(Courtesy of Great Pacific Iron Works.)

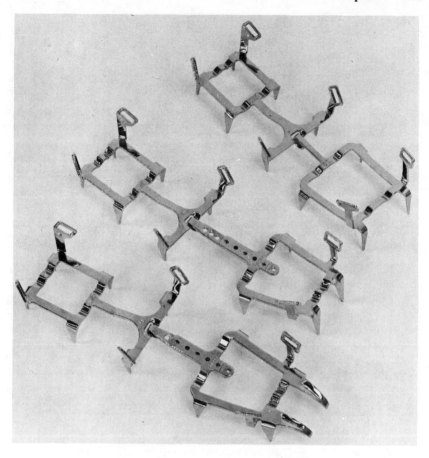

SMC crampons. (Courtesy of
Seattle Manufacturing Corporation.)

SMC also produces two flexible crampons, one with front points, the other, a ten-point model, without them. The flexible crampon is excellent for general, technical ice climbing. The ten-point is designed for glacial travel.

Clog crampons, manufactured in Wales and imported by Climb High in Burlington, Vermont, were originally designed for the British Mount Everest Expedition. Made

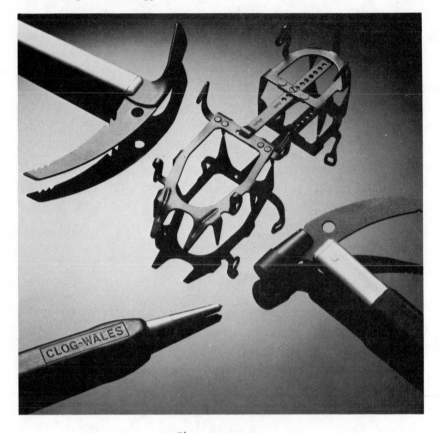

Clog crampons.
(Courtesy of Climb High, Inc.)

from chrome-moly steel, all the bending operations to shape the Clog crampons are performed hot, and each crampon is finished by Clogwyn's blacksmiths. These are excellent crampons for general mountaineering purposes— both technical ice and glacial climbing. They are well suited for use with a flexible boot. They are available in medium and large sizes.

Simond produces two adjustable crampons that are almost indestructable; both are made from superhardened steel. The points keep their rigidity and sharpness longer than any other crampons we have used. The Simond Super Jorasses crampons are unequalled in their handling characteristics on rock. They are suitable for both flexible and rigid boots. The Simond Makalu is similar to the Super Jorasses but has extremely slanted front points. The bottom two points tilt forward and actually lean in against the ice, providing very good support on vertical ice bulges. The Makalu is the better of the two crampons for American water ice. We've used the Simond crampons on New England ice for the last two seasons and feel they are the best performing flexible crampons available.

Lowe Alpine Systems has introduced a completely innovative crampon for vertical water ice called the Foot Fang. Its design is startlingly different from any of its

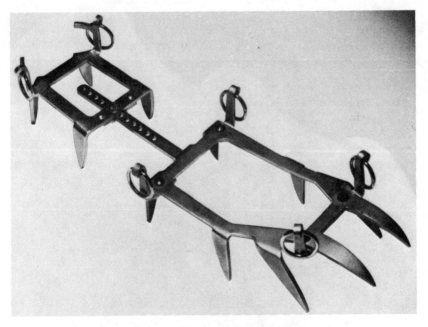

Simond Makalu crampons.
(Courtesy of ETS Claudius Simond et fils.)

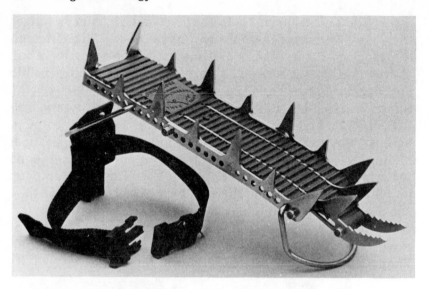

This page and opposite,
the Foot Fang.
(Courtesy of
Lowe Alpine Systems.)

predecessors; it looks something like a section of the Verrazanno Narrows bridge or the train trestle near Frankenstein Cliffs or a piece of an erector set. The Foot Fang has sixteen bottom spikes and two prominent front points. Ingeniously, the Lowe brothers took the principle of the ice axe and added teeth to the front points so that they are serrated to provide more secure footholds in the ice. The Foot Fangs are not attached to boots by straps, but by a metal clip in front, which locks onto the welt of the boot. A heel support in back locks the crampon in place and has a safety strap attached to fit around the ankle of the boot. Since it is absolutely rigid, it can be used with either a flexible or a rigid boot with no fear of bending or breaking.

The Foot Fang is definitely the crampon of the future, designed specifically for climbing vertical water ice.

9

Ropes

A Little Background History

Ropes have been used by mountaineers for centuries, but it wasn't until the late 1800s that climbers began tying themselves together with rope as a safety measure. Hemp was the material used, and it was hemp rope that Edmund Whymper used in his ascent of the Matterhorn in 1865. The tragedy that befell Whymper's party is well-known. During a fall on this first successful ascent of the Matterhorn, one of the hemp ropes broke, killing several members of the party.

While climbing ropes provided extra protection, the low breaking strength of hemp made them unreliable. The prevailing rule was, "The leader does not fall," for if the leader fell, the rope would surely break.

Hemp was replaced by nylon during World War II. A braided nylon climbing line called Mountainline was used by U.S. Army troops and, after the war, by civilian

Edelrid ropes.
(Courtesy of Robbins Mountaingear.)

climbers. Nylon solved problems of rope breakage, and climbers were able to climb with a freedom not earlier experienced.

In 1951 Edelrid, a German manufacturer, developed a stronger rope, also of nylon, called the Kernmantle rope. Unlike braided-line ropes, the Kernmantle consists of internally continuous strands of nylon filament covered with an outside sheath of woven nylon strands. This combination of inner and outer nylon is so constructed that it offers much better handling on rock, snow, and ice than the Mountainline. One of the problems with the twisted and braided Mountainline was that during a free rappel the climber would find himself spinning in space as the rope untwisted. The Mountainline is awkward to coil, whereas the Kernmantle is soft and supple—it doesn't kink. And the Kernmantle is better for tying knots than the Mountainline. Mountainline is still used, but is generally confined to instructional organizations whose needs for beginning climbers do not justify investing in expensive rope.

In 1966, Edelrid made the first water-repellant surface-coated rope, a wonderful benefit, particularly for winter climbers who no longer have to worry about their ropes icing up or becoming soggy. All manufacturers have since followed Edelrid's lead and offer fully waterproof ropes.

The Rivory Joanny rope company, instead of treating their rope with a water-repellant chemical, makes a waterproof rope by placing a plastic sheath between the outer Kernmantle and the internal cord. The plastic sheath is strong enough to withstand the test of a rappel or fall without ripping or breaking.

Choosing and Using Climbing Ropes

Climbers should have complete faith in their rope's ability to hold them in a fall. I myself know of no instance of a rope breaking during a climb. I do know of ropes that have been cut by sharp rock edges, or worn or frayed by rubbing against abrasive rock.

Climbing rope is usually available in three lengths: 120, 150, and 165 feet. The 120-foot rope is best suited for short crags and top-rope situations. On long cliffs and mountains, 120 feet of rope is not enough because the distance between secure belay attachment points, especially on rock and ice, is usually more than 120 feet. The normal length of a long pitch in technical climbing is 150 feet. On some ascents in Yosemite, the distance may be greater, and 165 feet of rope is required. It is very important to know the distance between pitches on established climbs.

Climbing rope is available in 9-, 10-, 11-, 11.5-, and 11.7-

millimeter diameters. The size best suited for most conditions of rock and ice climbing is 11 millimeters. For glacial climbing and snow work, a 9-millimeter rope is more than sufficient. The thicker rope is preferable for rock climbing because the roughness and abrasiveness of rock is hard on nylon.

A European "double rope" method of climbing requires two 150-foot, 9-millimeter ropes. The two ropes are used as one. They are clipped together into protection points. The two ropes provide insurance against the possibility of one of your ice tools or crampons accidentally cutting one of the ropes. I have lately been using the double rope technique not only on rock climbs but also on steep waterfall ice.

Always use the newest, strongest, and most trusted rope for leading a climb. In climbs where climbers switch leads, both ropes should be similar in quality.

All ropes now available in the United States meet the specifications of the UIAA (L'Union International des Association d'Alpinistes), an international body concerned with climbing safety. The UIAA has established test procedures and standards for climbing ropes. Simulated falls on ropes are made to test the strength of all rope. When a rope meets the UIAA fall test, it is certified and labeled. The UIAA label is not attached unless the rope has been tested to withstand a minimum of three UIAA controlled falls. The UIAA designates ropes according to the number of falls they have taken, the highest number so far being fourteen. However, I pay no attention to these designations because, in my opinion, if a rope has undergone a serious leader fall it has served its purpose and should not be used again. Multifall ropes are advantageous on long expedition climbs when climbers are limited to a small number of spare ropes; on such an expedition, a multifall rope might be needed. But as far as I know, expeditions and serious climbers all replace their ropes often, and particularly after a major fall. If you have used a rope for several seasons and feel it may be time to replace it, you are probably right. Trust your own judgment. You can save the rope for top roping or for climbing as a second.

Care and Maintenance

Try to keep your rope as clean as possible because ground-in grit can weaken nylon fibers, both outer and inner. Avoid stepping on a rope, as this will grind in small crystals of rock. If a rope is used in sandy areas, it should be washed after use.

The best way I know of to wash ropes is in lukewarm or cold water and Ivory Snow in a front-loading, nonagitating washer on gentle cycle. Spread the rope out on a lawn to dry or string it around your dorm room or hang it in a tree. Avoid drying it under direct sunlight.

Coil a rope loosely when it is not in use. Keep it away from direct sunlight and heat, and store it in a cool, dry area.

Some rope sheaths slip with use. If there is empty sheathing at the end of your climbing line, you may remove it by passing a heated knife over the end of the rope. Be sure to seal the end to prevent any inside strands from cracking, splitting, or coming undone. If your rope should be cut by a rock, the damaged part can be removed in the same manner.

Ropes can be affected by chemicals and acids. If the trunk of your car is as full of miscellaneous chemicals and greasy stuff as mine is, don't throw your rope there. Put it in a clean place.

A rope is by no means a long-term piece of equipment. But with proper and sensible care, you can maintain your rope to last as long and protect you as well as it was designed to.

Market Update

The developer of the Kernmantle rope, Edelrid, makes ropes for all types and degrees of climbing. I have used Edelrid ropes since I first started climbing. Their handling characteristics are second to none, and they show very little sign of wear even when used with jumars or rope ascenders.

In 1979, Edelrid introduced a newer and stronger rope called the Jumbo. It has been tested to withstand eleven to fourteen UIAA falls. It is a very heavy rope suitable for rough use.

The Classic Edelrid will withstand six UIAA falls. The 11-millimeter, 150-foot Classic weighs 7.1 pounds. The Edelrid Everdry, with the same specifications as the Classic, is treated with water-repellants that are guaranteed for the life of the rope. After prolonged use in wet snow, some water will seep through the Everdry but not enough to allow it to stiffen or freeze.

This year Edelrid has produced for Robbins Mountaingear a rope called the Royal Robbins Lifeline. It is 11.5 millimeters and comes in 150- and 165-foot lengths.

The Edelrid Dynaloc M is a high energy absorption rope with a low-impact force of 2,090 pounds. It weighs 7.4 pounds.

Royal Robbins also distributes an Edelrid called the Robbins Standard, economical in price but not in strength. It is a superior rope, available in 11 millimeter, 150-, 165,- and 300-foot spools. The weight of a 150-foot rope is 7.1 pounds.

Edelrid provides a handy informational and instructional pamphlet with each rope they sell.

Rocca ropes from West Germany have been used on rock faces and Alpine walls from the Rocky Mountains to the Andes and the Himalayas. They handle extremely well not only in rock and ice climbing but also in aid climbing when pendulums and traverses are frequently called for.

TECHNICAL SPECIFICATIONS

	Robbins Standard	Classic		Lifeline	Dynaloc L	M	Jumbo Everdry
Diameter (mm)	11	9	11	11.5	10	11	11.7
Weight per meter (grams)	70	51	70	75	60	69	82
Number of UIAA falls held	7	17	6	7	5	9	11-14
Impact force (Kg)	970	1050	1050	990	980	950	910
Impact force elongation (%)	23.4	20	21	20	20.7	24	21.5
Breaking elongation (%)	48	45	63	56	87	68	60
Static breaking strength (Kg)	2550	1620	2700	2870	1750	1900	3040
Elongation in use (%)	5.6	5.3	4.2	5.4	5.6	3	3.8

Specifications of Edelrid ropes.
(Courtesy of Robbins Mountaingear.)

There is no undue stretch of a Rocca rope. The Rocca 11-millimeter rope withstands over four UIAA falls. It is available in 9-, 10-, and 11-millimeter sizes for technical ascents. The Superdry waterproof model, in 10- and 11-millimeter sizes, absorbs very little water. Rocca manufactures accessory cordage rope in 4- to 8-millimeter diameters.

Mammut is a highly respected Swiss manufacturer of nylon cordage and ropes. The Mammut rope has very good handling characteristics and abrasion resistance to sharp rocks. It is available in a Standard 11-millimeter rope and a Superdry. The length is 45 meters or 148 feet, and 50 meters or 164 feet.

Mammut's Dynamic Standard rope is available in 9- and 10.5-millimeter sizes, in both 45- and 50-meter lengths. The Mammut ropes are excellent. Their handling characteristics are superb, and the outer sheath wears wonderfully well. Mammut also manufactures accessory cordage in 4- to 8-millimeter diameters, on 400-foot spools.

Lowe Alpine Systems imports Omniflex ropes, manufactured in France to their specifications. They are available in three models. The Dark Rainbow, in 9- to 11-millimeter, 150 and 165 feet, is tested to a nine fall factor. The Waterproof Dark Rainbow has the same specifications.

Properties Chart Rocca Cordage

Diameter (s)	mm	8	7	6	5	4
Static tensile strength	lbs.	3,548	2,424	1,781	1,146	727
Weight per meter	grams	35	30	24	16	10
Colors		Gold	Blue	Orange Green	Red	Purple

Properties Chart Rocca Kernmantle Rope

	Unit					
Diameter(s)	mm	11	11	10	10	9
Special characteristics		Energetic Superdry		Superdry		
UIAA **SINGLE** rope drop tests withstood		7	5	2	2	
UIAA **DOUBLE** rope drop tests withstood				10 +	10 +	10
UIAA peak impact force	pounds	2,038	2,160	2,204	2,204	2,270
Tensile strength over 10mm edge	kp	1,560	1,840	1,320	1,320	1.180
Elongation at rupture	%	66	45	51	51	45
Elongation with 80 kp static load	%	4.7	3.5	4.6	4.6	5.4
UIAA knotability	mm	9.75	9.00	7.50	7.50	6.50
Static tensile strength	pounds	4,210	6,226	4,430	4,430	3,934
Weight per meter	grams	74.8	71	63	60	47
Colors		blue	red blue gold	green	red blue gold	red blue gold

Rocca ropes and specifications.
(Courtesy of Forrest Mountaineering.)

Mammut ropes. (Courtesy
of Seattle Manufacturing Corporation.

The Duodess, with the same specifications, is bicolored,
with a color change at the midpoint of the rope; and 18
feet at each end of the rope is also a different color. The
color changes help you find the middle of the rope for
belaying and let you know how much rope is already out.

The most popular rope in the Eastern United States is
the Edelweiss, an Austrian rope available in three models:
the Extreme, the Compact, and the Extreme Everdry. The
Edelweiss ropes are compact and have a tightly woven
mantle over the core. Edelweiss maintains its own sophisticated testing laboratories where their ropes are put

Technical Data on Edelweiss Energy Ropes

Rope Construction: *Kernmantel*   Core Construction: *Bundlecore*

TYPE:	11mm EXTREM	11mm COMPACT	9mm EXTREM	11mm EXTREM (Everdry)	9mm EXTREM (Everdry)
1. UIAA Tested as	Single R.	Single R.	Double R.	Single R.	Double R.
2. Diameter (mm)	10.9	10.6	8.9	10.6	8.9
3. Weight Per Meter (m/g)	72.5	67.9	50.6	72.5	50.6
4. Weight Per 150 Ft. (lbs)	7.2	6.7	5.0	7.2	5.0
5. Flexibility in Knotting (mm)	9.5	9.5	7.5	9.5	7.5
6. Sheath Slippage (mm)	15	20	20	15	20
7. Working Elongation (%)	5	5	4	5	4
8. Static Tensile Strength (kp)	2250	2100	1680	2250	1680
9. Rupture Over an Edge (kp)	1650	1427	1200	1650	1200
10. Working Capacity Over an Edge (5mm±0.1mm) (mkp/m)	287	262	293	287	293
11. Breaking Elongation Over an Edge (%)	42	42	50	42	50
12. Impact Force (kp)	975	950	1100	975	1100
13. Number of Falls Held UIAA Drop Test	9	5	20	9	20

*Specifications of Edelweiss ropes.
(Courtesy of Climb High, Inc.)*

through twenty-two different tests before they are offered for sale. The technical advisor for Edelweiss, Reinhold Messner, has contributed greatly to their success. There is accessory cordage available in 3- to 9-millimeter diameters, called Edelweiss Power rope. The 9-millimeter Power rope is not recommended for lead climbing; the Edelweiss Extreme 9-millimeter rope is climbing line.

Joanny ropes have been used in technical climbing since 1946 and have been available in America for a number of years. Joanny ropes are of superior quality with excellent handling characteristics in cold weather.

Joanny's 9-millimeter, water-resistant, double rope is guaranteed to be waterproof for the life of the rope. Joanny ropes are available in 150- and 300-foot lengths, and are bicolored.

Interalp, a well-known and highly respected Italian manufacturer, makes rope with a very soft outer Kernmantle shell, available in 9- and 11-millimeter sizes, in both 150- and 165-foot lengths.

One of the new additions to the American market is the Gold Mantle, distributed by the Cordage Group of the Columbian Rope Company. Gold Mantle is the most inexpensive Kernmantle rope on the market and has good handling characteristics.

The Elite-Bernina rope has been available for the past several years through the Kalmar Trading Corporation. It is available in 9- and 11-millimeter sizes, in both waterproof and standard models. Elite-Bernina ropes have extremely soft outside sheaths, which unfortunately get very fuzzy very quickly. However, this only looks and feels bad; it does not affect the performance of the rope in any way. The standard model does tend to pick up snow and ice, making it a very kinky rope. The waterproof model is a much better choice.

10

Ascending Devices

When equipment hauling is necessary on big walls of over 1,000 feet, rope ascending devices are necessary. There are a wide range of these available. We've used many different types over the past ten years and have a few favorites, which we will discuss. This discussion will necessarily be biased and subjective, but we hope not unfair or misleading.

A Little Background History

Rope ascending devices came into use as a logical step in the progression of technical climbing equipment. During the first ascents of the Nose of El Cap in Yosemite Valley, mechanical ascending devices were unheard of. Prusik knots were used. Prusik knots are slow, uncomfortable, and often extremely difficult to use. They are still valuable in glacial climbing, especially where major crevasses are present, and provide good emergency backup in rappels. But for hauling equipment and seconding on long climbs, the prusik knot is undesirable and not much used anymore.

Care and Maintenance

Be careful to protect your ascending devices from direct hammer blows and make sure they are not dropped. If they are subjected to forceful abuse in any way, check to see that none of their parts are damaged.

If tape is used to attach a carabiner to an ascending device, it should be checked frequently and replaced often, or as soon as wear is visible.

When using ascenders on any icy rope, take care to clear away the ice as much as possible before sliding the ascender up.

To keep the cam gates of the ascender free, lubricate them with penetrating oil such as WD-40. Be careful to wipe them very well so no residue of oil remains; the oil will mess up your rope.

Use ascending devices wisely and correctly, making sure that both are always clipped to the body at all times. This is particularly important. If one of them accidentally becomes disengaged from the rope, you will still be protected by the second.

Market Update

The Jumar ascender, made by the Jumar Company in Switzerland, is the most popular and widely used rope ascending device in the world. It is a camming device which locks onto the rope and stays locked until disengaged by a lever. The lever releases the cam, which opens to its fullest. Early Jumars were made with a very lightweight, cast-aluminum body. The uniformity of treatment in the casting process left many of the handles on the

Jumar ascender on rope.

Jumar body weak. With continued use, side impact load, or if dropped, hairline fractures formed, leading to Jumar failures. The new Jumars have been reworked so that this is no longer a danger. The design and the diameter of the handle have also been improved, making a stronger and safer product. The grip has been enlarged to allow for the use of thick woolen mittens, a definite improvement. The new Jumar has an increased area of contact with the rope; this makes it safer for use on traverses than the earlier model.

Webbing should be used to attach the carabiner to the Jumar. There are several methods of tying in. A good discussion of these methods is included in Royal Robbins's *Advanced Rockcraft*.

In 1974 I had the opportunity to field-test the original Clog Expedition Ascenders when they were first imported into the United States. They have undergone several changes since then, and the current Expedition Ascender is probably the safest and strongest ascending device one can buy. I've since used Clog Ascenders on solo climbs of Grades V and VI.

The Clog Ascender has a molded grip that allows the hand to rest comfortably during long ascents. The original Clogs had carabiner holes for attachment directly to the handles, in the new model recommended attachment is by tying 1-inch tubular webbing to the bottom of the ascender. The accompanying diagram of a Clog Ascender is of the original model. Today, the webbing should be tied where the carabiner was attached to the old Ascender. Everything else is the same. An important feature is a 2-inch section of bent aluminum in the area where the cam and rope meet, providing greater security and strength during horizontal traverses, cleaning aid climbs, and Jumars. (Jumaring, by the way, is now the generic term for ascending ropes.)

The Gibbs Ascender is the only model which completely encircles the rope, requiring removal and separation of

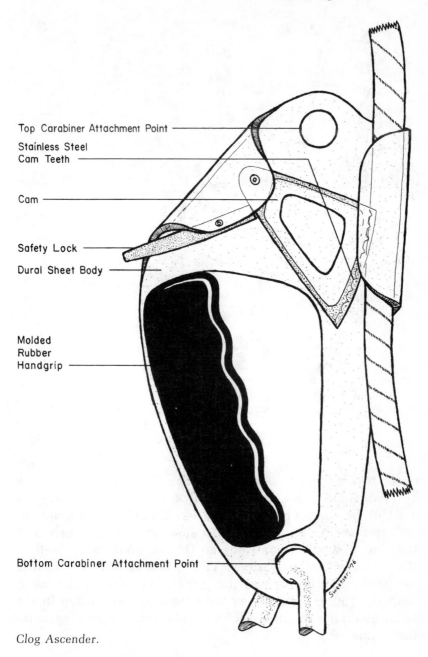

Top Carabiner Attachment Point

Stainless Steel
Cam Teeth

Cam

Safety Lock

Dural Sheet Body

Molded
Rubber
Handgrip

Bottom Carabiner Attachment Point

Clog Ascender.

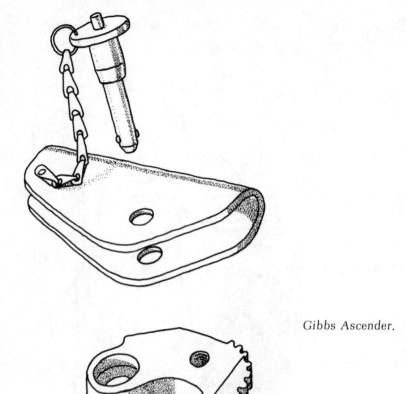

Gibbs Ascender.

parts to disengage it from the rope. The Gibbs is used a great deal in caving and is well suited for free standing and for free ascents from caverns. The Gibbs is good for mountaineering expeditions because once it is attached to the line it won't come undone. It also holds very well to wet, muddy, and icy ropes. The Gibbs is not as versatile for hauling equipment as the Jumars and Clogs. However, both the Jumars and Clogs are prone to ice buildup in the teeth of their camming devices. This is not a problem with the Gibbs.

11

Packs and Haul Bags

Choosing and Using a Pack

The technical climber uses many mechanical aids. But regardless of what aids or equipment the climber uses, he must carry them in a pack on his back. There are so many packs available on today's market, it would be impossible to adequately discuss each one here. Instead, I will recommend and discuss only four packs, the ones which I believe are the best currently available.

The packs I have selected were all specially designed for serious mountaineering use. For a day climb, just about any pack will do. On a longer climb, when you carry your gear for days, and sometimes weeks, it is extremely important to choose the best pack available for that purpose.

Care and Maintenance

Climbing packs are usually treated very roughly and get

very dirty. Most packs can be washed. The easiest way is to scrub the pack out of doors with Ivory Snow, a soft bristle brush, and a hose. After scrubbing, the pack should be hung up to air dry.

Small repairs can be made by your local cobbler, by a Speedy Stitcher, or with needle and thread. If your pack has leather patches that lose their color, waterproof dye will restore the color. However, we recommend that you choose a bag with a minimum amount of leather. Leather dries and rots in time. Even oiling will not keep it in good shape for many years of use.

Market Update

In the late 1960s, a new body contour pack was introduced by Don Jensen. This is an up-to-date version of the contoured pack used by military parachute jumpers, which has a tubular frame shaped more or less to the parachuter's back. These are still available from Army Surplus stores in some areas.

Jensen's pack requires careful packing to hold the weight of the bag very close to the body. This is a great asset on technical ice climbs, long rock climbs, and long expeditions. The Jensen pack is available in several different models to meet the needs of the individual climber. I have used a Jensen pack for many years and find it a most comfortable pack.

Lowe Alpine Systems has a versatile line of packs, the best of which is the Expedition Bag. The Expedition has a special harness system that allows adjustment not only in the shoulders and torso but also at the waist. It has a single, large compartment to carry a great deal of bulky or oversized equipment. There is a bivouac extension that pulls up and extends well above the waist. The top pocket is easy to get to for removal of rainwear, camera lenses, or whatever you want to reach in the middle of a climb. This

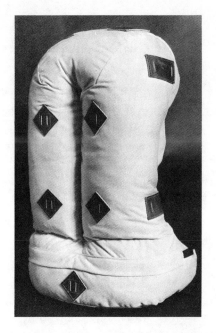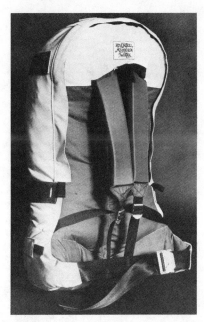

Original Jensen pack, front and back views.
(Courtesy of Rivendell Mountain Works.)

is a great pack for expeditions, but it is also good for general mountaineering.

Karrimor is an English firm whose technical equipment advisor was Dougal Haston. Until his death in a skiing accident, he was one of the five best Alpinists, with many notable ascents to his record. Using the basic design of the Vallot pack, Haston designed a bag for Karrimor called the Alpiniste. Haston incorporated several new design features into his pack, including a full zippered opening in the front of the single large compartment. This arrangement allows the climber to reach in by just opening one zipper. The zipper is covered with a placket that closes with Velcro.

The lower suspension system of the Alpiniste serves as

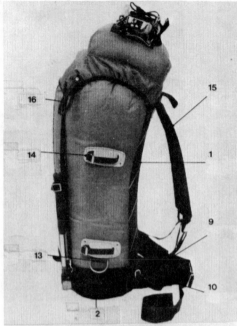

The dominant features of the Haston Alpiniste sac are:-

1. An "Aergo" chevron back panel gives an anatomic shape with increased ventilation giving a cooler carry. The back panel is made from closed cell foam for use as a bivi pad but has an overlay of softer foam for carrying comfort.

2. Double nylon reinforced base. Dougal would not contemplate a leather base under any circumstances because of its absorbancy (thus ice and snow adhere) and its greater weight.

3. The capacity: weight ratio is much better than the old Alpiniste.

4. The sac is ergonomic, i.e. anatomic (shaped) and sized (available in sizes 50,55 and 60).

5. It is extendable by use of the long bivi to 80-90 litres capacity. The long flap straps should be crossed over the top of the extended load. There are 2 pairs of buckles to enable the flap to be pulled down over the front of the sac when it is half empty. The flap pocket should be left empty when using in this way.

6. The extension has a full length zip with a double puller.

7. The extension zip runs half way down the sac and can thus be used for ventilation into the bivi or access to the lower part of the sac.

8. The velcro facing over the zip adds double security to the fastening.

9. The padded hip belt wings are of great assistance for heavy load carrying up to a climb.

10. The "emergency" ice axe belt can be used either as it is or with a hammer holster threaded on. It can be used for glacier crossings and ski mountaineering. Not normally used in a climbing situation because the belt is wrapped out of the way leaving the lower torso free for the climbing harness.

11. Tunnel which holds the hip belt out of the way as described above.

12. Double ice axe fittings to hold a full complement of todays ice climbing implements.

13. Gear attachment ring.

14. Ski and pocket attachment fittings. No modern alpine sac is complete without these.

15. Wide super soft foam shoulder harness.

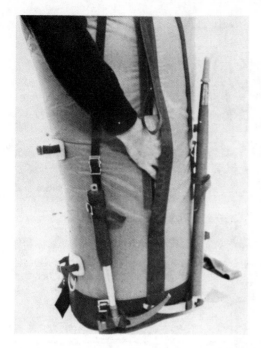 

Extension zip   Top with extended load

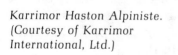

Karrimor Haston Alpiniste.
(Courtesy of Karrimor
International, Ltd.)

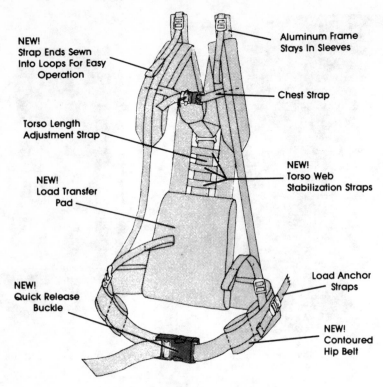

NEW!
Strap Ends Sewn
Into Loops For Easy
Operation

Aluminum Frame
Stays In Sleeves

Chest Strap

Torso Length
Adjustment Strap

NEW!
Torso Web
Stabilization Straps

NEW!
Load Transfer
Pad

NEW!
Quick Release
Buckle

Load Anchor
Straps

NEW!
Contoured
Hip Belt

Lowe Expedition Bag harness system.
(Courtesy of Lowe Alpine Systems.)

a tool carrying sling. Two ice axes can be slipped into
each of the gear attachment rings on the side of the bag. A
hammer and axe can be hung from the waist belt. Crampon straps are provided on the top of the pack, and two
ice axes can be tied very securely to the back.

The Alpiniste is designed to be used in conjunction with
a conventional climbing harness; the Whillans Sit Harness
is a perfect mate for it. It has a pullout bivouac extension
that comes well above the waist. The Alpiniste is made of

lightweight, waterproof nylon. Sewn into the back are foam panels that prevent sharp implements from jabbing the climber in the back. It is available in three separate sizes, 50, 55, and 60 centimeters.

If a climber is involved in serious mountaineering and is only going to own one pack for winter or Alpine climbing, the Haston Alpiniste would get my vote because it is one of the most sophisticated and advanced packs available. However, it is hard to find in the United States. It is currently imported by Dartmouth Outdoor Sports and International Mountain Equipment in North Conway, New Hampshire. After ordering, I waited almost a year to receive mine. But it was definitely worth the wait.

The best French mountaineering packs are produced by the Millet Company. The Millet Huandoy 558 is an excellent pack. It has a large compartment with overhead entry, and a small lower compartment constructed of PVC-coated polyester material. The entire pack is waterproof. It has two side pockets and a double top-closure, which allows rainwear, important maps, etc., to be reached easily. The convenient pockets also keep camera lenses and equipment out of harm's way. Two sleeves for skis are provided on the side of the pack. It has a slipout bivouac sheet and back padding made from vertically sewn, foam panels. The Millet Huandoy is very well suited for ice climbing, steep rock climbing, and heavy mountaineering where large loads of equipment must be carried.

While all of these packs are extremely well designed and well made, we have found that for big-wall climbing they do not wear well and are too fragile for hauling equipment up the long walls. For big-wall climbing, one sometimes needs more than 125 pounds of gear. Since it's too difficult to carry all this on your back during the actual climb, sturdy haul bags are used. These can be carried on your back both on the approach to the climb

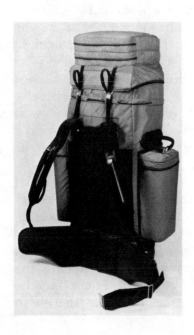

This page and opposite,
*Millet Huandoy. (Courtesy of
Sacs Millet S.A.)*

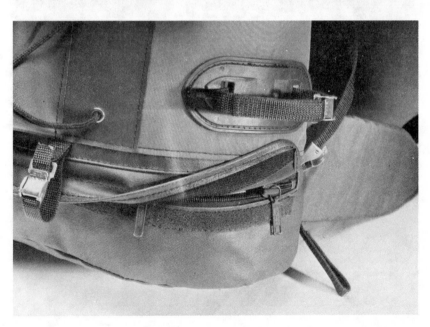

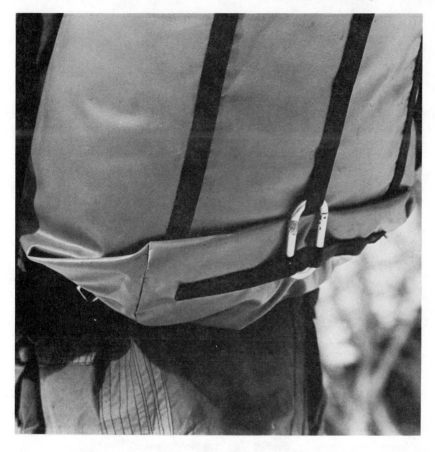

Left and above, *Forrest Grade VI Hauling Bag.*
(Courtesy of Forrest Mountaineering.)

and on the descent. For the ascent, they are hauled with a conventional pulley system. Any of the packs previously discussed would not survive this hauling.

Forrest Mountaineering produces a very good bag called the Grade VI Hauling Bag, which has seen numerous ascents of El Cap and of walls in South America. The Millet firm in France also produces an excellent haul sack.

Its inverted cone shape makes it very easy to pull over precipices and rock projections. Both of these bags have excellent shoulder suspension systems, and we recommend them for your big wall climbs.

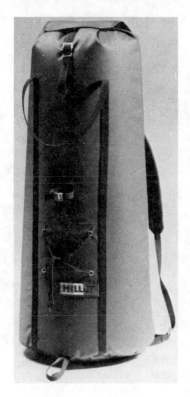

Millet haul sack.
(Courtesy of Sacs Millet S.A.)

12

Clothing and Sleeping Bags

We've discussed the products of high technology that now permit mountaineers to scale higher mountains and to seek more challenging peaks. Space-age technology has not been applied to tools and equipment only; it is responsible for the development of warmer, drier, and better clothing for mountaineers and climbers.

It would require at least one complete volume for an adequate discussion of the many and varied items of clothing available to today's climbers. I'd like to discuss only a few brand new items that are particularly significant.

Gore-Tex

A major development in new clothing materials was the introduction, about five years ago, of Gore-Tex, a breathable yet totally waterproof fabric. Gore-Tex was originally developed for use in heart surgery, thus its breathability and waterproof properties. It is wonderfully applicable to sportswear. Clothing made of Gore-Tex allows the active sportsman to perspire freely; the perspiration escapes, allowing him to keep cool and dry. Yet Gore-Tex blocks moisture penetration from the outside. Many products are now being constructed from Gore-Tex, including wind and rain pants, mountaineering jackets, mitten shells, overboots, and, the latest addition, sleeping bags.

The benefits of a Gore-Tex sleeping bag are many. It allows the Alpine climber to survive a forced bivouac in a snow cave, on an exposed mountain ledge, or on a glacier during a storm. The Gore-Tex outer covering eliminates the need for carrying a waterproof shell to protect your bag.

One of the experiences familiar to all Alpine climbers is waking on a cold, wintry morning to a downpour of condensation that has accumulated on the tent walls during the night. The climber and his sleeping bag are drenched; he is left cold and miserable at the beginning of a day's climb. With a Gore-Tex covered bag, this problem becomes past history.

Gore-Tex fabric consists of three layers of material—an inside Gore-Tex membrane between two layers of nylon. Because it has three layers, Gore-Tex fabric is more wind resistant than conventional rip-stop nylon or standard nylon sleeping-bag material.

Marmot Mountain Works of Grand Junction, Colorado, was perhaps the first specialty mountaineering outfitter to manufacture a down-filled sleeping bag with a Gore-Tex outer cover. The Marmot Pocket Gopher bag is wonderfully light, weighing only 3 pounds. The down fill itself weighs only 25 ounces. The Pocket Gopher will keep you toasty warm and dry down to a temperature of zero. Marmot Mountain Works is an exceptionally respected

Marmot Gore-Tex sleeping bags.
(Courtesy of Marmot Mountain Works.)

manufacturer, and their down Gore-Tex bags are of superior quality.

Cedar River Mountaineering makes Gore-Tex bags with Polar Guard fill rather than down fill. Polar Guard, a synthetic insulation, has the advantage of being considerably less expensive than down, which brings the Cedar River bags within economical reach of most climbers.

Two models of Polar Guard Gore-Tex bags by Cedar River are the Stampede and the Cascade. The Stampede will keep you warm to 10 degrees Fahrenheit. If you use it along with other clothing and a down parka, the bag could keep you warm in temperatures well below zero. The Cascade model is guaranteed to keep you warm to 10 degrees below zero and is an excellent expedition bag.

The Vista Company of England uses polyester pile fill to

Cedar River Gore-Tex bag.
(Courtesy of Cedar River Mountaineering, Inc.)

Vista Eskimo bag.
(Courtesy of Vista Thermal Products, Ltd.)

insulate their sleeping bags, and an outer covering of waterproof nylon and Gore-Tex panels. The Vista Eskimo bag was used by the British K2 assault team in 1978 and has been used on many expeditions to the Arctic Circle.

Another Vista bag, the Shearwater, is an excellent Alpine bivouac bag. The Shearwater is the lightest pile-

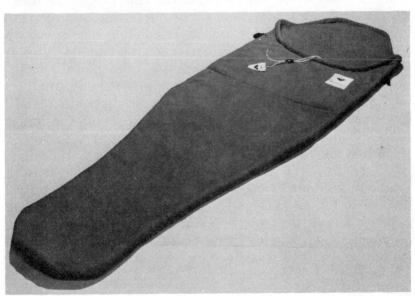

Vista Shearwater bag.
(Courtesy of Vista Thermal Products, Ltd.)

filled bag I know of. It is extremely small and compact and is equally at home on mountain climbs and backpacking expeditions.

The important thing to know about Gore-Tex is that the membrane can be contaminated by body oils and oily dirt. Gore-Tex products should be laundered in soap rather than detergent. For particularly dirty stains, the manufacturer suggests using denatured alcohol, followed immediately by a thorough rinse. To guarantee complete waterproofing of a Gore-Tex product, the seams must be sealed with seam sealer.

Pile

The British have been using fiber pile for warmth for a long time. Used originally by British seamen and fishermen, it was much cheaper and warmer than the traditional, Irish-knit fisherman's sweater. Eventually, British climbers began using it, and it is catching on here, fast. Almost every small American specialty manufacturer is now producing clothing made of fiber pile—pants, jackets, mittens, and socks. Again, there are too many products and too many manufacturers to discuss them all. We feel the ones included here represent the state of the art in fiber-pile products.

In Britain, the Tog Textral Manufacturing Corporation, Ltd., makes the Tog 24 pile-lined climbing jacket, with or without a hood. The Tog pile is the tightest and softest I've seen. It's an excellent jacket for crag climbing. When worn underneath a Gore-Tex outer jacket, it makes an extremely warm and waterproof combination for ice climbing. By itself it is a good all-around jacket. The outer surface of the Tog does not fuzz and pill as easily as some of the others.

Vista makes a heavy pile jacket, also used by the 1978 British K2 expedition, and by many other high-altitude expeditions. It is very thick and very warm. I bought my Vista K2 jacket two years ago because I liked the long,

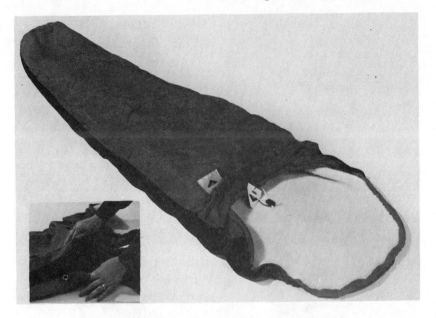

Vista Beaver bag.
(Courtesy of Vista Thermal Products, Ltd.)

Tog 24 climbing jacket.
(Courtesy of Tog Textral Manufacturing Company, Ltd.)

Vista K2 jacket.
(Courtesy of Vista
Thermal Products, Ltd.)

Synergy Works pile
jacket. (Courtesy of
Synergy Works.)

one-inch pile, which is the thickest I've seen. The Vista jacket is extra long, covering the seat of my pants, which keeps me warm during ice climbs in those fierce New Hampshire winters. The jacket has not lost any of its loft, but the exterior is rather fuzzy and pilled, an inevitable occurrence with pile.

The best American-made pile jackets are made by Early Winters Limited in Seattle. Early Winters produces a layered system—a pull-over with a zippered neck; a vest with a full chest zipper; and a long-sleeved, high-collared, lightweight jacket—all made of pile. The three garments are designed and sized to be worn together. The combination of the three will rival the warmth and snug feeling of a Vista parka, and offer the advantage of having three separate items for independent wear.

Synergy Works produces an excellent pile jacket, with a high rolled collar and full underarm zippers to allow ventilation during heavy exercise.

Pile is easy to care for. It can be washed and should not be dry cleaned. One characteristic of pile is that it will pill and fuzz. This affects only the look, not the function or warmth, of the garment. Like Polar Guard, pile immediately regains its loft when dried. It is, therefore, superior to down as an insulator in wet conditions. A combination of pile for warmth and Gore-Tex for waterproofing is outstanding.

Space-Age Jackets

The best jackets I've seen to date, of any variety, are produced by Millet in France.

The Millet model 2110 and model 2160 were both designed with the technical cooperation and advice of Reinhold Messner. The 2110 is a high-altitude, Himalayan expedition parka; the 2160 is for Alpine climbing. The design and construction of these two jackets allows complete freedom of movement in technical climbing. They are well ventilated.

Even more exciting is Millet's newest offering, the model 2600 T2. It is an outstanding parka of absolutely superior quality in every detail and facet of design and construction. An original Millet design, this parka is made of material that reflects 80 percent of natural body heat back to the body. It has several layers of material. The inside layer is a tightly woven, completely windproof nylon. The next layer is a reflective insulating material similar to Thinsulate (it may actually be Thinsulate; I don't know). Woven around the insulating material is an additional man-made, polyester insulation layer to help maintain dead air space and reflect heat. The next layer is triple

*Millet Model 2110.
(Courtesy of
PGB Associates.)*

laminated, waterproof Gore-Tex. The outside is an abrasion-resistant, breathable nylon and cotton fabric.

The jacket has a two-way zipper with a very high neck, a built-in hood, knitted cuffs, a drawstring at waist and bottom. Besides being stunningly designed, the jacket allows full freedom of movement and has two ventilation holes under the arms to prevent overheating. If worn over a sweater or pile garment, the jacket could keep a climber warm and dry through an Arctic bivouac.

The 2600 T2 was introduced in 1979. Unfortunately, it is not yet available here in the States. It may be ordered directly from the manufacturer. It is an extremely expensive parka, but well worth every penny.

Appendix I
Recommended Books

Advanced Rockcraft. Royal Robbins. Glendale, Calif.: La Siesta Press, 1973.

Basic Mountaineering. Henry I. Mandolf. San Diego, Calif.: San Diego Chapter of the Sierra Club, 1975.

Basic Rockcraft. Royal Robbins. Glendale, Calif.: La Siesta Press, 1971.

Bergsteign. R. C. Aleith. Scottsdale, Arizona: Arizona Mountaineering Club, 1971.

The Climber's Sourcebook. Anne Schneider and Steven Schneider. New York: Anchor Press/Doubleday, 1976.

Climbing Ice. Yvon Chouinard. San Francisco, Calif.: Sierra Club Books, 1978.

The Field Book of Mountaineering and Rock Climbing. Tom Lyman and Bill Riviere. New York: Winchester Press, 1975.

First Steps to Climbing. George D. Abraham. New York: Robert M. McBride Company, 1925.

The Ice Experience. Jeff Lowe. Chicago: Contemporary Books, 1979.

Manual of American Mountaineering. Kenneth A. Henderson (ed.). New York: American Alpine Club, 1941.

Mountain Climbing for Beginners. Mike Banks. Briarcliff Manor, New York: Stein and Day, 1978.

Mountaineering. Alan Blackshaw. New York: Penguin Books, 1975.

Mountaineering: A Manual for Teachers and Instructors. D. T. Roscoe. Transatlantic Press, 1976.

Mountaineering: The Freedom of the Hills. Harvey Manning, Chairman of Editors. Seattle, Wash.: The Mountaineers, 1960.

On Ice, Rock, Snow. Gaston Rebuffat. New York: Oxford University Press, 1971.

Appendix II
Addresses of Manufacturers, Importers, Distributors

Asolo
PLB International, Inc.
8141 West I 70 Frontage
    Rd. No.
Arvada, Colorado 80002
(303) 425-1200

Campbell Mountaineering,
    Inc.
P. O. B. 9339
Madison, Wisconsin 53715
(608) 274-5373

Peter Carman
Uptown Sewing, Inc.
P. O. B. 700
Jackson, Wyoming 83001

Cedar River
    Mountaineering, Inc.
John Hiffman
P. O. B. 347
Enumclaw, Washington
    98022
(206) 825-4456

Chouinard Equipment for
Alpinists
P. O. B. 150
Ventura, California 93001
(800) 235-3371

Climb High, Inc.
227 Main Street
Burlington, Vermont 05401
(802) 864-4122

Clogwyn Climbing Gear,
Ltd.
Clwt y Bont, Deiniolen
Gwynedd, North Wales
LL55 3DE
(Tel.) Llanberis 551 (STD-
028-682)

Colorado Mountain
Industries Corporation
P. O. B. 535
Franklin, West Virginia
26807

The Cordage Group
Columbian Rope Company
Auburn, New York 13021
(315) 253-3211

Dartmouth Outdoor Sports,
Inc.
P. O. B. 960
Hanover, New Hampshire
03755
(603) 448-1300

Donner Mountain
Corporation
2110 Fifth Street
Berkeley, California 94710
(415) 843-6705

Early Winters, Ltd.
110 Prefontaine Place South
Seattle, Washington 98104
(206) 284-4979

Euro-Linea S.N.C.
Giuseppe Cereghini
38100 Trento
Via Perini, 54, Italy
0461/984920

Fabiano Shoe Company,
Inc.
850 Sumner Street
South Boston,
Massachusetts 02127

Forrest Mountaineering
1517 Platte Street
Denver, Colorado 80202
(303) 433-3372

The Gendarme
Mouth of Seneca, Box 53
West Virginia 26884

Gibbs Products
854 Padley Street
Salt Lake City, Utah 84108
(801) 582-5872

Jardine Enterprises
1339 North Prospect
Colorado Springs, Colorado
80903
(303) 632-8152

Karrimor International, Ltd.
Avenue Parade Accrington
Lancashire, England

Kastinger
Anderson & Thompson Ski
Company
455 Andover Park East
Seattle, Washington 98188
(206) 575-0390

Ed Leeper
Salina Star Route
Boulder, Colorado 80302
(303) 442-3773

Liberty Mountain Sports
Liberty Organization
4116 La Crescenta Avenue
La Crescenta, California
91214
(800) 423-2666
(213) 248-0618

Lowe Alpine Systems
Box 189
Lafayette, Colorado 80026
(303) 665-9220

Marmot Mountain Works
331 South 13th Street
Grand Junction, Colorado
81501
(303) 243-2339

Millet—U.S.A.
c/o Lisa Airhart
310 East 46th Street
New York, New York 10017
(212) 682-6731

Mountain Safety Research,
Inc.
631 South 96th Street
Seattle, Washington 98108
(206) 762-6750

Pak Foam Products
390 Pine Street
Pawtucket, Rhode Island
02862
(401) 726-2360

Recreational Equipment,
Inc.
1525 Eleventh Avenue
Seattle, Washington 98122
(206) 323-8333

Rivory Joanny S.A.
Jean-Joseph Durand
Rue du Pont Fournas
42402 St. Chamond, France
(77) 22.02.48

Robbins Mountaingear
Box 4536
Modesto, California 95352
(209) 529-6913

Rooster Mountaineering
Box 157
Aspen, Colorado 81611

Sacs Millet S.A.
36, Av De Chambery
Boite Postale 109
74003 Annecy Cedex France
(50) 51.11.59

Seattle Manufacturing
    Corporation
12880 Northrup Way
Bellevue, Washington 98005
(206) 883-0334

Simond
Ets Claudius Simond & Fils
Les Bossons 74400
    Chamonix
France
(50) 53.02.58

Snowdon Mouldings
Snowdon Street
Llanberis, North Wales
Great Britain

Synergy Works
255 Fourth Street
Oakland, California 94607
(415) OK CLIMB

Tog 24
Textral Manufacturing
    Company, Ltd.
Unit 171, Walton Summit
Bomber Bridge, Preston
England
Preston 311787

Troll Safety Equipment,
    Ltd.
Spring Mill
Uppermill, Nr. Oldham OL
    3 6AA
England
Saddleworth (045 77) 2120
    and 6189

Vasque Ascender II Boots
Red Wing Shoe Company
Red Wing, Minnesota 55066

Vista Thermal Products,
    Ltd.
106 Eldon Street, Haxby
    Road
York, Y03 7NH England
York 20490

Index